Aircraft & Legend
JUNKERS JÜ52

HEINZ J. NOWARRA

Foulis

Haynes

A **FOULIS** Aviation Book

ISBN 0 85429 592 5

First published 1986

English language edition published 1987

Published by:
Haynes Publishing Group
Sparkford, Nr. Yeovil, Somerset BA22 7JJ,
England

Haynes Publications Inc.
861 Lawrence Drive, Newbury Park,
California 91320, USA

British Library Cataloguing in Publication Data
Nowarra, Heinz J.
  JU 52 : aircraft & legend
  1. Junkers JU-52 (Transport plane)
  I. Title
  623.74'63   TL686.J8
  ISBN 0-85429-592-5

Library of Congress catalog card number 87-80605

Editor: Mansur Darlington
Cover illustration: David Parker
Printed in England by: J.H. Haynes & Co.

Contents

Introduction

Ever since my first flight in a Junkers F 13 on Easter Monday 1926, Junkers aeroplanes have again and again determined the course of my life. As a pupil I used to watch at the Berlin-Tempelhof airport for new Junkers types to make their appearance. At the International Aviation Exhibition (ILA) of 1928 I admired the 'flying restaurant car' Junkers G 31. Later, Tempelhof became the almost daily destination of bicycle excursions, by then with a camera. After 1933 the look of Berlin airport was determined by the Ju 52; at the busiest times of the day, the rush hour as it is called to-day, around 4 o'clock in the afternoon, one saw little else but Ju 52s on the runway.

During the war and until 1945 it was my task to ensure the supply of spares for Ju 88s and Ju 188s and after the war I met many people who had not only flown the Ju 52 but had, in some way or another, been responsible for them: Flugkapitän Otto Brauer, who had piloted nearly all Junkers types from the F 13 to the Ju 290; Generaloberst a. D. Alfred Keller, former chief of Luftflotte 1, who had been responsible for maintaining the airlift to Demyansk, and his Lufttransportführer (LTF), Oberst Morzik, had fulfilled the task in exemplary fashion using Ju 52s; and finally, Oberstabsingenieur Richard Scholz, who had been involved in the build-up of the Luftwaffe from the beginning and who was, at the end of the war, responsible for M & S Luftflotte 5, and who flew many miles in his Ju 52 PI + 0A. I, myself, got to know the type when Ju 52 combat planes came to Leipzig to collect spare parts.

All this gave me the idea that I would, one day, write a book about the Ju 52 and its history, which would start with the F 13 and end with the French AAC1 in 1956.

With this work I have received much help from many people; my special thanks are due to:

Oberst a. D. Beckmann
Rudolf R. Blümert, Vienna
G. Balaguer, Bandung
Pierre Cortet, Marseilles
H.P. Dabrowski, Hanover
Deutsche Lufthansa AG, Cologne
Deutsche Forschungs- und Versuchsanstalt für Luft- und Raumfahrt, Porz
Jean Devaix, Bougival
Dr Roberto Gentilli, Florence
Juan Antonio Guerrero, Barcelona
Dr Heinrich Göers, Osnabrück
Rainer Haufschild, Berlin
MBB-Werk, Bremen
Knut Maesel, Kristiansand
Peter Petrick, Berlin
Thijs Postma, Hoofddorp
Rupert Reisinger, Vienna
Herluf Rasmussen, Braedstrup
Bruce Robertson, London
Helmut Roosenboom, Bremen
Jay P. Spenser, Smithsonian Institution, Washington DC
South African Airlines, Johannesburg
Scandinavian Airlines System, Stockholm
Fritz Trenkle, Fürstenfeldbruck
Johan Visser, Monnickendam
Bo Widfeldt, Nässjö

From F 13 to G 31

After the First World War the position of the German aircraft industry looked a hopeless one, since the Armistice and Peace Treaty of Versailles forbade Germany any form of aircraft construction until 1922. Professor Hugo Junkers, in charge of the Dessau aircraft works, rightly decided to change the emphasis of their activity from the needs of the military to civil aviation, the post-war growth of which would be inevitable. As a result of this decision and after extensive preliminary studies, headed by Junkers director Otto Reuter, the world's first all-metal cabin aircraft was built in January 1919 in spite of the Treaty's prohibitions. Its introduction was all the more remarkable because civil aviation in the victorious countries still took place exclusively in provisionally adapted war planes. One of the preliminary versions, the Junkers 12, became J 13, later known as F 13.

Development work was deliberately not concentrated on peak performance but on the most economical long-term performance. The design called for a low-wing monoplane with cantilever wings and tubular spars; dual controls and trim facilities; and safe accommodation of the passengers, protected from the airstream in a spacious enclosed cabin with windows. These were the main features of this, the world's first true civil aviation machine, and, broadly, they still apply today.

Construction work for this machine started on 10 February 1919 and was completed on 20 June 1919; on 25 July the first F 13 started on its first flight, with test pilot Monz at the controls. Different versions of the name of this first machine exist: in initial reports it was described as *Anneliese,* in memory of the wife of Prince Leopold of Anhalt-Dessau. On 18 July 1919 it was registered as D-183 *Hertha,* under the works number 531. This first machine was powered by a Mercedes D 111, of 160 hp, but was later given several new engines. When in 1920 the then aviation register was replaced by a new one, the plane was given the new registration number D-1, which it retained until 1940. Between April 1924 and January 1926 D-1 flew for the Bayerischer Luft-Lloyd and was subsequently transferred to Deutsche Lufthansa, established on 20 June 1926. The book's author, at the age of thirteen, made his first flight ever on Easter Monday 1926 in this aeroplane. D-1 was used by Lufthansa for regular flights until 1938 and was later taken over by the subsidiary Hansa-Flugdienst, which had been established to carry out special flights and round trips. In June 1940 the machine was transferred to the Luftwaffe and flew, at least until November 1940, for the pilot training school A/B1 at Görlitz. Nothing further is known about its subsequent history.

On 1 October 1920 Director Reuter engaged Dipl. Ing. Ernst Zindel for the construction bureau, and his name was afterwards linked with the future development of all Junkers aeroplanes. After Reuter's death Professor Mader assumed responsibility not only for the development of engines but also for the construction bureau. Apart from Zindel it employed the engineers Stärke and Pinkert, the designers Scheller and Reinike, and, from Forschungsanstalt Prof. Junkers (Junker's research establishment), Dipl. Ing., later Professor, Georg Madelung as well as Dipl. Ing. Steigenberger and Dipl. Ing. Weissenfels.

During the following years the F 13 was repeatedly improved and equipped with various engines. Among these were the following: BMW 111a, BMW IV, BMW Va, Junkers L2 and L5, Armstrong-Siddeley Puma and Jaguar, and Pratt & Whitney Wasp. After 322 aeroplanes had been built, production of the F 13 ceased in 1932. Apart from Germany, the F 13 was flown in the following countries: Belgium, Bolivia, Brazil,

Canada, Colombia, Czechoslavakia, Estonia, Finland, Hungary, Italy, Poland, Portugal, Romania, Spain, South Africa, Sweden, Switzerland and the USSR. Eight planes were supplied to the USA and a number of machines were built under licence under the name Junkers-Larsen JL 6.

The construction of metal aeroplanes started primarily in Germany. Without the aeroplanes built by Junkers, Dornier and Rohrbach, which were subsequently exported all over the world, the development of modern all-metal aeroplanes would have started considerably later.

Professor Hugo Junkers, who was the moving spirit behind all the early Junkers aeroplanes, was a democrat through and through and had little time for the military. Nevertheless all his machines, developed for civil aviation, were again and again modified and flown for military purposes.

It was not just to the F 13 that this fate befell, it was shared by all subsequent models from the G 23 to Ju 52. The F 13 was fitted with a machine gun support behind the pilot's seat and flown as a military aeroplane in the USSR and Persia.

As early as 1923 it became apparent that the single-engine F 13 with its passenger capacity of four to five persons was no longer sufficient for the rapidly growing civil aviation requirements. It thus became necessary to increase passenger capacity to 9 - 11 persons and to use more than one engine so that the safety of the passengers was ensured, even were one engine to fail. Ernst Zindel was asked initially to undertake a number of draft studies and, subsequently, the design of the final version, as well as the design drawings for the individual units. His staff included, among others, the engineers Ing. Starke, Haseloff, Freundel and Dipl. Ing. Pohlmann, who later became head of the design office at Blohm & Voss. At the beginning of design work the restrictions imposed by the Versailles treaty — limiting engine power until 1926 — were still enforced, so that the first machine of the new type G 23, later known as G 24, had to be fitted

with one centrally-mounted BMW IIIa engine of 185 hp, and two wing-mounted Mercedes engines, each of 120 hp. Series construction, on the other hand, could only take place initially with three BMW IIIa engines, which remained from First World War stocks, when this engine was primarily used in the single-seater Fokker DVII. Since only a few engines of this type remained, Junkers developed a slightly improved version of the BMW IIIa, which was subsequently supplied under the name Junkers L2 and used in the F 13 and G 23, as well as the G 24. The difference between the G 23 and G 24 was only slight. It is certain, however, that all machines built between 1924 and 1926 were known as G 23, and that this model is not mentioned subsequently. Apart from the above-mentioned prototype, four G 23s were supplied to the Swedish airline authorities, and four further ones to the Swiss company Ad Astra Aero. The general public was introduced to the G 23 in the summer of 1925 through a round trip from Danzig-Malmö via Copenhagen-Schiphol-Zurich-Vienna and Berlin.

The lack of clarity that surrounds the G 23/24 programme is probably due to the fact that at the same time Junkers built, in a Swedish subsidiary, AB Flygindustri, Linhamn, not only the G 23 – production for which was just about to start – but also the derived bomber R 42, listed in the Junkers type list as K 30. In addition to the prototype, the G 23 was made in two versions, the G 23dL, with a Junkers L2 as central engine and two Mercedes DI as wing engines. The seaplane version G 23dW had Mercedes D IIIa engines, more powerful by 40 hp, as outer engines. Production of the G 24 at Dessau and Linhamn started in 1926. Around sixty G 24s were built in twenty different variations, as well as at least six R 42s. A further seven G 24s were ordered by the German government. These machines were used for training the crews of the, at the time highly secret, naval and army pilot units then being established. Some were registered with Deutsche Verkehrsflieger-schule, others with the firm Severa. The R 42 was known in the USS R as the G-1. Other machines of this type of bomber were supplied to Turkey and South America. As a straightforward civil aviation plane the G 24 was supplied to the following countries: Austria, Brazil, Finland, Greece, Italy, Poland, Spain, Sweden and Switzerland. Lufthansa used the G 24 for regular flights until 1934, other countries considerably longer; the last G 24 flew in Brazil in 1938.

The following main versions of the G 24 were built:

G 24e, 3 Junkers L5s of 280/310 hp, flying weight 5500-5700 kg.

G 24ba, 3 Junkers L2s of 265 hp, flying weight 6000-6300 kg.

G 24be, 1 L5 and 2 L2s, flying weight 6000-6300 kg.

G 24de, 3 L5s, flying weight 6000-6300 kg.

G 24fe similar to G 24de, different engine installation, flying weight 6000-6500 kg.

These versions were built between 1924 and 1926. In 1927/28 the following were added:

G 24ge, 3 L5s, closed cockpit, flying weight 6500-7000 kg.

G 24gu, 1 L5 425 hp and 2 L5s 310 hp, trial only.

G 24nao, 3 Jupiters of 510 hp, trial only.

The last and most powerful version was the G 24he, 3 L5s, flying weight 7000 kg; as float-plane version, flying weight 7600 kg, built in 1929.

In 1928 a three-engine G 24 was converted into a single-engine freight plane, which was powered by a BMW V1 of 450/600 hp. This aeroplane had a flying weight of 4000 kg and was known as G 24ko. A further ten G 24s were converted to single-engine civil aviation planes, some being fitted with a BMW V1 engine, others with BMW VIIs of 600 hp. The BMW VII version was known as F 24kau. In 1929 the F 24 was fitted with a heavy Jumo 4 diesel engine of 650 hp. The F 24 and G 24 can be regarded as immediate forerunners to the Ju 52. The G 31 is no more than an intermediate stage.

Under the Rapallo treaty of 1925 the G 24 had to be converted to the K 30/R 42 bomber and this meant that Junkers was now constantly engaged in building aeroplanes in both civil and military versions, for example A 20/R2, A 32/K 39, S 36/K 37, A 35/K 53, G 38/K 51. In order to be able to develop the necessary weapons systems, Junkers set up the 'Weapons Development' unit which was headed by Oberst von Merkatz, who had undertaken similar tasks until 1918 for the armaments authorities of the army. The official head of the 'Design Group-Development' was Ing. Steuerlein, who was in charge of this group until 1945. His closest colleague was Ing. Gremser. The modification of the G 24 to the type K 30 and its military equipment took place at Linhamn. The Junkers Type K 30 was offered by AB Flygindustri, in their literature, as AB Flygindustri R 42. The name Junkers did not appear in the company's prospectuses.

Efforts were made by Junkers to utilize each aeroplane type for both civil and military purposes. This led to tensions between Junkers and the military authorities of the Reich. Since 1924/25 the German military had tried to develop, in utmost secret, a peace-time air force. The first step consisted in training future flight personnel. For this purpose the Deutsche Verkehrsfliegerschule (DVS) was founded, to train pilots for the army, while the firms Aerosport and Severa were set up by the navy. When, after the foundation of Deutsche Lufthansa (DLH) on 6 January 1926, Erhard Milch became one of the managers of DLH, this was the beginning of close co-operation between the Reichswehrministerium (War Ministry) and DLH.

After the establishment of the German flight base at Lipetsk in the USSR Junkers F 13 were used as liaison aeroplanes. The G 24 of the DLH had, from the onset, been earmarked as bombers but were initially used only as training aircraft by DVS and Severa. In 1929 Technische Fliegergruppe (the aviation technical department) within the Heereswaffenamt (WaL) (the weapons procurement office) under Hauptmann Volkmann requested the development of different aeroplane types for different uses. This was in direct contrast to the views held by the Junkers manager Sachsenberg. He did not think that anything but a standard aeroplane was required which would, basically, correspond to the K 30/R 32. The Reichswehr regarded Sachsenberg's request as simply a measure aimed at promoting the sale of Junkers production aeroplanes. Within the Reichswehr itself different opinions existed about the value of a civil aviation or freight plane as a bomber.

It was thought that a single-seater fighter plane was indispensable for a 'peace-time airforce'. Although Junkers had built an all-metal single-seater fighter in 1917/18, its use as such was limited. The H 22 fighter built after the war for the USSR, had been a failure. Although there were plans for the G 24 of the DLH to be used as a provisional bomber, it was thought that the Dornier Do freight plane would be more suitable for this purpose. Junkers, consequently, was excluded from the air armament plans. By the summer of 1925 the number of Lufthansa air passengers had risen to such an extent that the capacity of the G 24 with its nine to eleven seats was no longer adequate. Moreover, Lufthansa wanted to give its passengers greater comfort. As a result Junkers developed the G 31, which was based on the primary sections of the G 24, in particular the main plane structure; it, too, had three engines. Professor Mader put the modification work into the hands of Dipl. Ing. Hofmann, who had only recently joined Junkers, and who was later to specialize in the design of propellers. The prototype, works number 3000, was completed in 1926 and registered under the number D-1073. This aeroplane was powered with three Junkers L5 engines, each of 280/310 hp. A completely new feature of the G 31 was the so-called 'auxiliary equipment section', fitted into a special compartment, which virtually corresponds with the present day flight engi-

neer's station. The first flight of D-1073 took place in spring 1926. Because of its box shape the G 31 had a somewhat clumsy appearance. The L5 engines were soon replaced by Gnome-Rhône Jupiter engines, each of 510 hp. It was in this form that the G 31 was exhibited at the 1928 International Aviation Exhibition (ILA) where it was particularly impressive next to the Röhrbach Romar. In addition to its crew of three the G 31 normally carried fifteen passengers. Only D-1310, christened the *Herman Köhl,* after the successful transatlantic pilot, still had only eleven seats, but it had a greater range and interior fittings that earned it the name 'flying restaurant car'.

On 24 May 1928 a G 31 became the one thousandth Junkers aeroplane to be built at Dessau. The successful transatlantic flight with a Junkers W 33 inspired an Australian pilot, who was looking for gold in New Guinea, to buy a Junkers W 34 as a freight plane for his tools and equipment, and the mined gold. Other major mining companies operated in New Guinea and they, too, were faced with difficult territory and population problems. This gave Charles A. Banks, president of the Canadian Placer-Development Inc., the idea to enquire whether Junkers could produce aeroplanes large enough to fly two chain-and-bucket excavators weighing 1000 tonnes, as well as all their accessories, over the mountains and forests of New Guinea to the mines. The excavator producers agreed to supply the excavators in components weighing no more than 3000 kg. There were still a few unsold G 31 at Dessau. The problem of stowing the excavator units, some of which were 7m long, in the body of the G 31 was solved by detaching the rear end of the G 31, inserting the section and then re-attaching the rear section. Junkers was given the order to supply three G 31, two for the newly established Bulolo Gold Dredging Cie. and one for New Guinea Airways. Between January and November 1931 the G 31 took components to the mines and was able, from July 1932 onwards, to fly back the gold mined with their help. The cargo of up to 540 tonnes per month exceeded, in 1931, the amounts carried by any other airfreight company world-wide. In all, fifteen G 31s were built. The experiences gained during the development and use of the G 24 and G 31 finally led to the development of the Ju 52.

Professor Hugo Junkers, the father of the modern all-metal aeroplane.

Dipl. Ing. Ernst Zindel, the creator of Junkers' Ju 52.

Junkers F 13, the world's first all-metal civil aviation aircraft, works number 531.

Junkers F 13, modified as a military aircraft with machine gun emplacement, in Persia.

Junkers F 13W, works number 786, belonging to Severa, a company belonging to the Reichsmarine.

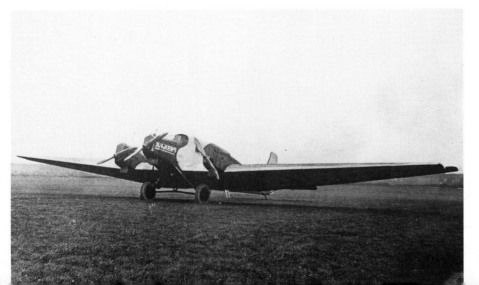

The first Junkers G 24.

13

Junkers G 24W of the Finnish Aero O/Y, previously K-SALC, works number 919.

AB Flygindustri R42 (modified Junkers G 24).

AB Flygindustri R 42W (modified Junkers G 24W).

The first Junkers G 31,
works number 3002,
became D-1310.

14648

Junkers G 31, D-1310,
with new engines, the
Gnome-Rhône Jupiter.

Luxury for Lufthansa
passengers as early as
1928.

Kabine des Großflugzeuges Typ Junkers G 31.   Speisewagen Betrieb.

Junkers G 31 D-1427,
works number 3004,
destroyed by fire in
1928.

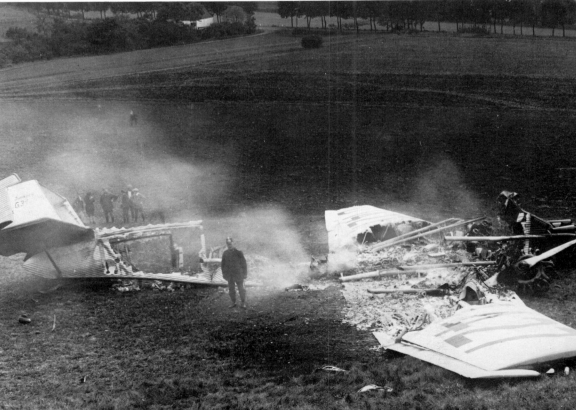

The single-engine J 52

In 1928 the design bureau of Junkers-Werke was given a new task of great significance and impact, the design and execution of which were placed in the hands of Dipl. Ing. Ernst Zindel. Zindel had overall responsibility of the entire development of the new J 52 aircraft, later known as Ju 52. He himself has written a detailed report on the reasons leading to the development of the Ju 52:

After the merger, in 1926, of Aero-Lloyd and Junkers-Luftverkehrs AG, (until then the two main competing German civil aviation companies), and the establishment of a single German state-subsidized aviation organization, Deutsche Lufthansa, Junkers and those of its aviation experts that had not been taken on by Lufthansa – Sachsenberg, Kaumann, Weyl and Bongers – no longer had any immediate influence on aviation events, with the exception of some foreign involvement.

Junkers and its own experts tried to find new and better ways of expanding aviation and of making economical use of the aeroplane, by far the fastest means of transport which was, moreover, independent of costly and time-consuming road or rail networks and which opened up hitherto unrecognized prospects for linking countries and peoples. Junkers had aimed, from the beginning, at independent air traffic without state subsidies. In contrast to general opinion on passenger air transport the old experts of Junkers-Luftverkehrs AG, and in particular the former head of the department Technik-Zentralwerftleitung Dipl. Ing. Weyl as well as Dipl.-Volkswirt Bongers (he was after the Second World War co-founder of the Federal Republic of Germany's new Lufthansa and for many years in charge of its economic affairs) were of the opinion that it would be possible to realize a fully independent economic operation. This opinion was based on experience with mixed passenger and freight air transport in Persia and New Guinea (where Weyl had been in charge for a number of years) as well as of detailed traffic/cost studies involving large-scale air freight, especially in little-developed countries.

They succeeded in firing the imagination of Professor Junkers and in convincing him of the good prospects of their project. It was, however, necessary to use a new specially designed and constructed aeroplane that could meet the needs and demands of economical air freight, especially in those countries that were, in those days, relatively underdeveloped both technically and in terms of traffic: it would have to be cheap to buy, economical to operate, easy and undemanding to maintain with a high payload, of at least 2000 kg; it would have to be simple to fly and maintain, so that demands on the crew and maintenance personnel would be low. Take-off and landing speeds would have to be moderate, and the aeroplane would have to be suitable for grass runways. In order to achieve the target of low purchase price and maintenance, the traffic experts recommended the single-engine version (provided that reliability of operation was ensured) as being sufficient for air freight as long as the machine could take off and land on grass runways. This meant at the same time that the aeroplane could, in this form, only be used for freight purposes. This was exactly what the people in charge of the old Junkers-Luftverkehr wanted. They were afraid that the best solution for airfreight traffic could not be achieved if the basic design and construction incorporated the necessary requirements for a single-engine passenger aircraft.

For those in charge at Junkers-Flugzeugwerk of the marketing of aeroplanes and the design department the problem was an entirely different one: their old customers, DLH and numerous foreign airlines urgently needed this new and more powerful aeroplane since the old three-engine G 24s dating back to 1924 were by now out of date, while machines developed by other companies were no adequate replacement and did not meet the increased demands of future air transport with regard to performance, reliability or safety; nor were their passenger capacity and comfort sufficient. In other words, Lufthansa and other airlines urgently needed a new more powerful commercial aircraft. This new aeroplane required for European and intercontinental scheduled passenger flights had to produce a considerably improved flight performance, in particular higher cruising speeds and maximum height as well as safety in flight, and this could only be provided by a multi-engine aeroplane, and one with adequate performance reserves; at the same time the required features included first-rate flight characteristics especially during bad weather and poor visibility, so that timetables could be conformed to despite much reduced flying times. If Junkers wished to avoid the loss of its existing markets as a supplier for a number of important airlines and regain its position as the main supplier of DLH, the management of Junkers-Flugzeugwerk had to introduce a commercial aeroplane which met all modern requirements with regard to performance, operational safety, and economy. This market and its anticipated demand were relatively easy to assess. By contrast, the question whether, and to what extent, plans of extensive airfreight could be realized in the near future was entirely open. In effect, the vital interests of the manufacturers and the hopes of the old air transport representatives were almost irreconcilable. Those arguments that favoured the interests of the enterprise as a whole eventually won the day. When the new aeroplane, which received the type designation J 52, was eventually designed and first constructed at the end of 1929, efforts were made to meet the requirements of Junkers-Luftverkehr in full with the initial single-

engine 'freight version' while at the same time laying the foundations on the basis of which a standard passenger aeroplane meeting all the necessary requirements could be developed. We succeeded in designing a satisfactory and uniform basic design for fuselage, wings and tail planes for both purposes, even though the design for a passenger aeroplane would have resulted in a slightly more favourable solution (number of passengers, cabin size). The fact that later on the multi-engine version became generally accepted for both passenger and freight machines was due to changes in use. The idea of independent air transport and freight alone was far ahead of the air transport concepts of the time and did not materialize until about thirty years later.

After we had carefully studied a number of possible solutions we undertook a survey of several interested parties, including the main airlines as well as the managers of flight and transport departments, in order to ascertain which requirements existed for a new passenger and freight aircraft and their opinions on our design.

In order to implement the airfreight operations planned by Junkers the firm Luftfrako Internationales Luftfracht-und Maklerkontor Air Express GmbH was set up, headed by Professor Junkers' son-in-law Hajo Folkerts. Consequently the first version of the new type was built in the form of a single-engine freight version. Initially the 650/800 hp Junkers L88 engine was intended as the power unit. But since its development had not been completed, a BMW VIIaU of 685 hp was used instead. The basic concept was the same as with all other previous Junkers aeroplanes: a cantilever monoplane with low-set wings and a corrugated metal skin. The single-engine freight version was distinguished by a large loading hatch, 1.6m wide and 1.5m high, with a corresponding loading ramp at the rear end of the fuselage side, freely accessible behind the trailing edge of the wings, and a laterally arranged flap, the lower end of which was used as a loading ramp. In addition, the fuselage ceiling was fitted with a 1.5 x 1.2 m loading hatch for the loading of heavy or bulky loads from above by means of a crane. The flight personnel had access from the freight compartment by a door in the cockpit aft bulkhead. As with previous types, the wing was fitted with high-lift flaps and ailerons to provide maximum lift during take-off and landing.

This first Ju 52, works number 4001, made its maiden flight on 11 September 1930, piloted by Flugkapitän Zimmermann. Control difficulties resulted in an enlargement of the rudder unit and an additional counterweight for the horizontal tail surfaces. Apart from Zimmermann, Flugkapitän Gothe and the flight test engineers Hoppe and Preuschoff were also involved in further tests. On 6 December 1930 the machine was moved to the Deutsche Versuchsanstalt für Luftfahrt (DVL) (the aeronautical experimental institute) of Berlin-Adlershof. Because of modifications requested by DVL the prototype test was not completed until 10 February 1931. The aeroplane received the registration number D-1974. Even at that early stage the military interest of this machine became apparent. A member of the French Embassy as well as two engineers of the Reichswehrministerium inspected the machine in an attempt to ascertain its suitability for its military use. One of them was the future Generalingenieur der Luftwaffe Lucht.

When devising the new Ju 52 Zindel intended, after much thought and experience gained with the G 24 and G 31 passenger versions, to develop a three-engine model. He commented: 'The three-engine version represented, at least for engines of the size under discussion and the prevailing operational conditions, the best compromise between safety and economy. Externally, the aerodynamic design and basic structure of the fuselage was practically identical for single-engine and three-engine variants, the major strengthening components only had to be modified to take account of the increased flying weight and higher speeds of the three-engined versions, as did the landing gear.'

Although it has been possible to dispel misgivings on the part of Lufthansa about monoplane construction, the company nevertheless rejected the single-engine Ju 52. After a planned long distance flight with D-1974 to Teheran had been cancelled, a 6000 km flight (Budapest-Bucharest-Sofia-Belgrade-Athens-Vienna-Prague) was a propaganda success but nevertheless brought no orders. After its return, D-1974 underwent intensive inspection and overhaul and, subsequently, further tests. On September 1931, piloted by works pilot Fritz Harder, the machine took off for the first time with the, by then available, Junkers L88 engine. It had been fitted with different wings, with a more marked sweep-back and greater taper. In addition it was fitted with a four-blade Heine wooden propeller with a diameter of 5.00m. After a number of modifications – amongst others a so-called 'diving safeguard' for the drag flaps had been installed – the Ju 52, now known as Ju 52ca, was again fitted with the BMW VIIuA and was cleared for flying on 18 January 1932. In the meantime, on 14 January 1931, the second Ju 52, works number 4002, had been completed. It was fitted with one of the first Armstrong-Siddely Leopard engines with a take-off performance of 800 hp, which later turned out to be a problem child. In March, despite all efforts, it refused to start. Only after an expert from the manufacturer's works had arrived did the Leopard deign to move; by then it was mid-April.

Around the same time D-1974 had been fitted, at the request of Lufthansa, with dummy wing-mounted engines so that measurements could be carried out to ascertain the performance reduction due to increased drag. This was the first step towards a three-engine Ju 52. Works number 4002 was meanwhile converted to a float-plane. The attachment of the 11.05m long floats was carried out at the Sachsenberg dockyard at Rosslau, a suburb of Dessau. This new form of the Ju 52 was known as Ju 52ci. Its first flight, under Flugkapitän Zimmermann, took place on 17 July 1931 on the Elbe near Rosslau. On 23 July the aeroplane was flown to Travemünde for prototype tests. The results of sea tests at grade three sea motion were unsatisfactory so that no final approval but only provisional approval under the number D-2133 was given. Junkers nevertheless planned to build ten further single-engine Ju 52s, namely those of works numbers 4003 – 4012. Of this series only those numbered 4003 – 4007 were supplied as single-engine versions. The other machines were converted to three-engine machines during construction. The construction of these machines had become possible as a result of options received from Bolivia, Iraq and New Guinea. Nevertheless, these options were not converted into firm orders. Then Canadian Airways Ltd ordered a Ju 52ca, works number 4006. This machine was shipped to Canada in October 1931, arrived in November, and was registered as Ju 52ce under the registration number CF-ARM. During the winter of 1931-32 it was put to immediate use as a supply machine for outlying trapper stations along the Hudson Bay. The machine remained in operation until 1942 when it was acquired by Canadian Pacific Airways and used until 1947. Zindel reports:

Although the machine used by Canadian Airways was eminently suitable for the special conditions and tasks, the single-engine freight version of the Ju 52 did not sell as well as anticipated, especially as the large scale airfreight plans of the old air transport experts of Junkers never materialized, simply because time and conditions were not ready for their underlying philosophy.' With this one exception, when a single-engine Ju 52 was actually used for its intended purpose as a freight carrier, all other aeroplanes were used for the development of the Kriegsmarine and Luftwaffe, despite the fact that these organizations operated under

disguise until 1935. The aircraft were modified on a number of occasions and given different markings.

As part of target practice for the Reichsmarine so-called tow-target shooting had been developed. The single-engine Ju 52 turned out to be a particularly suitable towing plane, capable of towing a 5 x 1m hollow drogue which formed a fast moving target over the surface of the water. For this purpose Luftdienst-Schleppstaffel (target towing squadron) Holtenau was established, and this was replaced, after 1935, by IV Luftdienstkommando Kiel-Holtenau. On 15 November 1935 works number 4007, with the marking D-UHYF, was the first of these planes to be used for this purpose. The necessary modifications to these single-engine towing Ju 52s, were carried out at the Junkers dockyard at Leipzig Mockau. D-1974, was also, after several modifications which included fitting of a Daimler-Benz DB 600, flown by the Schleppstaffel as D-UZYP. Works number 4002, D-2133, became D-USUS, and works number 4003 became D-USON. Works number 4005 was delivered in February 1933, as D-2356, to the test centre at Staaken of Reichsverband der Deutschen Luftfahrtindustrie, one of the camouflage addresses of the then still secret Luftwaffe. In contrast to all other Ju 52s it was fitted with a 600/800 hp BMW IXU and was known as JU 52cai. It burned out on 27 May 1933 after an emergency landing, due to a fire, near Rheinsberg.

The fate of works number 4004 registered in September 1932 as D-2317, was a particularly interesting one. Deutsche Verkehrsfliegerschule (DVS) was given as the operator of D-2317, in other words it was used for the secret training of future naval pilots. Since this included weapons training, D-2317 was flown, in December 1932, to Linhamn to AB Flygindustrie, where a torpedo launching device was fitted. At the same time the machine was given a Swedish registration number, SE-ADM. A similar operation had previously been carried out, when the courier aeroplane S 36 had been flown as an unarmed machine to Linham as D-1252, where it was fitted with gun turrets, flown initially as S-AABP, turned, after full armament, into SE-ABP and returned to Germany in 1934 as the long-range reconnaissance aircraft D-AMIX. SE-ADM returned to Germany in February 1933 where tests were carried out at Torpedo-Versuchsanstalt (TVA) Eckernförde, a naval weapons experimental establishment; these showed the necessity for modifications, which were once again carried out in Sweden. At the time it was said to have had the type designation K 45. However, this appears to have been no more than a camouflage number, since at the same time the German specialist press published a drawing of a single-engine Junkers F 45, which rather resembled the Junkers K 53. SE-ADM appears to have been more successful than the torpedo aeroplanes HE 7, HD 14, and HD 16 supplied by Heinkel. SE-ADM was primarily used in Sweden to test the Norwegian Horten torpedoes, which were intended for production under licence in Germany by the Schwarzkopf firm in Kiel; this however produced difficulties, since the torpedo type F5 turned out to be unsound. An improved type F5a was not available until after 1941. SE-ADM returned to Germany in 1935, was again refitted by Junkers Werft Leipzig (FWL) and subsequently flown at Kiel-Holtenau, once again as tow-target aircraft under the registration D-UBES for a number of years. This then concluded the chapter of the single-engine Ju 52.

The prototype Ju 52, works number 4001, photographed on the day of its maiden flight, 11 September 1930.

Junkers Ju 52ba, works number 4001,
was first introduced to the public at
Berlin-Tempelhof on 17 February 1931.

D-1974 with Junkers L88 engine and a
new type of propeller with a diameter of
5.0m after its Balkans round-trip in July
1931 at Vienna-Aspern.

Ju 52di, works number 4002, after its
interrupted sea trials in October 1931.

Works number 4002 as Ju 52ci during its sea trials at Travemünde, August 1931.

Works number 4004 was a Ju 52ce and was taken over in September 1932 by Deutsche Verkehrsflieger-schule (DVS). After 1933 it became D-UBES.

Top and side loading hatches of Ju 52ce.

23

Cockpit of Ju 52be, D-1974.

Freight compartment of the Ju 52be.

Entrance to the cockpit was from the side.

Oil-filled shock-absorber struts on the wing.

Swivelling tail wheel, also equipped with air/oil shock-absorber.

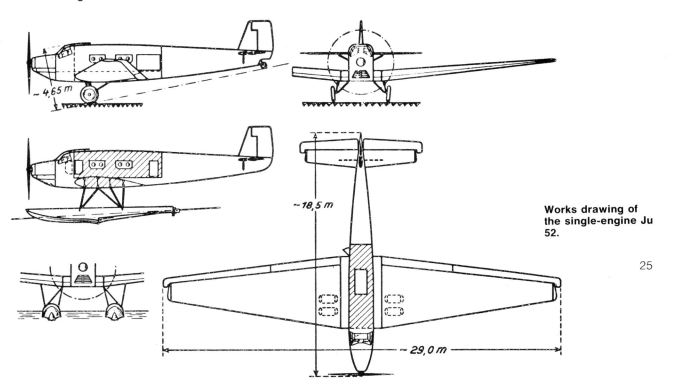

~ 4,65 m

~ 18,5 m

~ 29,0 m

Works drawing of the single-engine Ju 52.

25

The first three-engine Ju 52

Junkers had hoped to sell further single-engine Ju 52s and consequently work on works numbers 4008 to 4012 had proceeded so far that it was hoped to start the final assembly stage. But nobody wanted to buy single-engine planes; instead, for safety reasons, Lufthansa and others were looking for a new passenger plane with three engines. Urgent enquiries from South America had been submitted for such planes. In Colombia Fritz Hammer and Herr von Krohn had established a small aviation company as early as 1920 under the name Condor Syndicat. On 1 December 1927 the company moved its headquarters to Brazil. In its place Sociedad Colombiana des Transportes Aeras (SCADTA) was set up in Colombia with German capital and the important route Bogota-Baranquilla opened during the same year. This route passed along the Rio Magdalena and had been used by Hammer and von Krohn with Junkers F 13s fitted with floats.

The Colombian military forces were now looking for larger transport planes which could be used along this important route for the transport of troops and materials. Here, too, a machine with more than one engine was required. Junkers offered the three-engine JU 52 with floats and received an order for three machines. The decision had been made easier for the Colombian authorities by the fact that Lloyd Aereo Boliviano (LAB) had ordered two machines and these had been delivered within a short period of time, since the works numbers 4008 and 4009 had only to be converted to three engines. In the event, LAB did not receive these since Bolivia was at the time engaged in war against Paraguay, the so-called Gran Chaco War. Since this was fought in the jungle, supplies could only be moved by air. Here, the two JU 52s proved highly successful, even under difficult weather conditions, not only as transporters but also as makeshift bombers. The same was experienced several years later in Europe. Colombia received the JU 52s works numbers 4010, 4011 and 4012. The three machines were given the military numbers 621 – 623 and were stationed at Baranquilla. Three further machines, numbers 624, 625 and 626, were supplied by March 1934. Of these, four – namely 621, 622, 625 and 626 – were still in operation in February 1943, while 623 and 624 were lost as early as 1936 in Cabuyaro and Putumayo. One of the machines was seen at Bogota airport as late as 1966.

As a result of its satisfactory experiences with the first two machines Bolivia ordered two further ones, works numbers 4018 and 4061. After the end of the Gran Chaco War all four machines flew for Lloyd Aero Boliviano as passenger aircraft and instead of registration numbers were given the names *Juan del Valle*, *Huanuni*, *Chorolque* and *Bolivar*. In the first five machines the three BMW Hornet engines were fitted, as was then usual, by means of a cylindrical extension at the front of the fuselage, and one at the leading edge of each wing. The effect of this arrangement was described by Ernst Zindel:

The Ju 52/3m fitted with this arrangement first flew in spring 1931 and reached a maximum speed of around 230 km/h. The drag area corresponding to this speed was 5.8m² and was thus 2.3m² larger than that of the single-engine machines where this area amounted to 3.5m²; the latter had achieved a maximum speed of 200 km/h and a cruising speed of 178 km/h using a BMW VIIaU. The drag area of the three-engine model was primarily due to the high air resistance of the engines that were fully exposed to the airflow. Since the aim consisted in increasing adequately the maximum and

26

cruising speeds and in improving their performance figures compared with those of other models then in use, decisive action had to be taken in order to reduce the area.

A new principle, which had been evolved more than ten years earlier by Professor Junkers and for which a patent had been sought, was applied as a highly successful means of dealing with the outer engines arranged before the wing; the same principle was also used with great success by the Americans in conjunction with single-engine machines with relatively narrow fuselages, in particular fighter planes, and was known by the term NACA cowling. The reduction in drag area per outer engine amounted to about 0.9 m² each. Because of the proximity of the stout fuselage the cowl used on the central engine was less effective; here we had to use the so-called Townend ring which had been developed in Britain to reduce the drag of air-cooled cylinders, but was only of limited success.

Another major contribution towards reducing undesirable resistance took the form of streamlining the cladding of wheels and undercarriage struts. A combination of all these measures meant that the drag area of the three-engine JU 52 was reduced from its initial 5.8 m² to 3.4 m² and thus practically to the value of the single-engine machines.

At the same time maximum speed was increased from 230 to 270 km/h, and the economical cruising speed, which amounted to about two-thirds of the nominal performance, to 235 km/h. The reduction of the undercarriage drag was mainly due to experiments undertaken by Professor Junkers in his own wind tunnel. The optimum design of streamlined cowlings for the engine positioned in front of the fuselage and especially of the engines positioned in front of the wings as well as the correct form of the baffles required to guide the cooling air for the cylinders, was not achieved until after careful flight tests in close co-operation with the engine

makers BMW, so that the minimum of resistance and interference with the airflow coincided with adequate cooling in different flight conditions. Because of the asymmetrical flow over the upper and lower wings surfaces and the V-shaped leading edge of the wings, as well as the vortices created by the propellers, the flow conditions for the individual cylinders of the radial engines differed widely. The best solutions could only be found as a result of intensive experiments and measurements during flight, and these led eventually to the required formula.

As with the engine aerodynamic design of the aeroplane and the co-ordination of controls and control forces, which eventually resulted in excellent flight characteristics of the Ju 52, here, too, did the technical and scientific experiments bring optimum results. Because of the aerodynamically favourable design of the cowling, the air-cooled radial engines approached, with regard to their cooling and installed drag, the performance of the best water-cooled engines. The combination of favourable drag values, the relatively low weight of the engines, reliability and the relatively low price meant that nearly all transport planes used, until the introduction of the jet, air-cooled radial engines with this type of cowling.

The requirements of freight planes for a large loading area without cross members, easy access and loadability coincided with the need in passenger aircraft for comfortable passenger accommodation and large open areas for mail, freight and luggage, and resulted in the provision of several separate and convenient boarding and loading hatches.

The elevators and rudder unit were, as were the ailerons, of a special Junkers design, which had previously been used successfully in the considerably larger G 38. As a result, it became possible to keep all control forces relatively small – certainly within the operationally desirable limits – and to co-ordinate them successfully.

It can be said that:

– as a result of a relatively basic design and careful construction of all components,
– as a result of the combination of a highly developed lightweight construction with methods of progressive and experience-based engineering,
– as a result of easy accessibility and maintenance of all important components and not least
– as a result of high-quality materials and careful control methods during production and maintenance during operation,

it was possible to achieve a high degree of operational safety and reliability, which not only laid the foundation for the high degree of confidence shown by flying personnel and airline managements in the Ju 52 but also the confidence of the flying public in air transport as such.

Cancelled flights for technical reasons hardly ever occurred with the Ju 52, and even if, because of bad weather, no other machines were able to fly, the Ju 52 still started on its scheduled flights as long as somewhere in clouds, fog, or rain there remained a 'hole' through which it could land. *Tante Ju* ('Aunty Ju') as the plane was later called by both civil and military crews, soon became a symbol of safety and reliability. The success with which the compromise between performance, reliability and economy had been achieved with the Ju 52/3m was shown impressively by the result of the international Alpine flight competition for transport planes in 1932, when the young three-engine Ju 52/3m, which had only just taken to the air, ended up as clear winner; with a total of 1533 points it was convincingly ahead of its other competitors with 1044 and 522 points respectively.

This success and the deployment of the first ten production aeroplanes of the new and by then final version, for regular flights of Deutsche Lufthansa in 1932, marked the beginning of the great technical and economic success of the Ju 52/3m, which became, in subsequent years, the standard aircraft of many European and overseas air companies; more than 400 machines were used for transport and travel purposes, most of them with landing gear for land use and a smaller number fitted as floatplanes.

The maritime version had been fitted with new twin keel floats, whose aerodynamic and hydrodynamic shapes had been tested in the wind tunnel of the Junkers research institute. These floats were characterized by relatively low drag as well as favourable take-off and landing properties.

The first eight machines, which were built as three-engine models, and which can be regarded as a preliminary series for the Ju 52-3m, were given the works numbers 4013 to 4020. The first machine of this preliminary series went to Lufthansa. Works number 4013 was registered as D-2201 and given the name *Oswald Boelcke;* its type designation was Ju 52-3mce. The next machine, works number 4014, was originally fitted with an American Pratt & Witney Hornet engine and was designed so that its landing gear could be exchanged for floats. It was registered as OH-ALK and became part of the Finnish airline Aero O/Y fleet. The next machine, once again intended for Lufthansa, was works number 4015, registered as D-2202 and known by the name *Richthofen*. After these three Ju 52-3mce machines, works number 4016 was a special design for the President of the Fédération Aéronautique Internationale (FAI) Prince Bibesco; its central engine was an Hispano-Suiza 12Mb and the two wing engines were Hispano-Suiza 12Nb's. The central engine had an output of 750 hp, the others 575 hp each! This version was intended for private travel, and it was fitted with a luxury cabin and twin tail wheels. Designated Ju 52-3mba, it was registered as CV-FAI but was later used in regular service as YR-ABF. Works number 4017 was registered as SE-ADR for the Swedish AB Aerotransport and largely corresponded with the Finnish version. Works number 4018 went to Bolivia, was initially used for military purposes and later for civil flights by Lloyd Aereo Boliviano. Works number 4019 was registered as D-2468 for Lufthansa. With the exception of the one Ju 52-3mba these were all 'ce' versions. Works number 4020 started the next series, the Ju 52-3mfe, a transport aeroplane with three 550 hp BMW Hornet engines. This was an improved version with one-piece fuselage, cowled landing gear and outer engines with NACA cowls. The first models were delivered in 1933. They were succeeded, in 1934, by the series Ju 52-3mge, which began a new chapter in the history of the Ju 52.

Ju 52-3m, works number 4008, a modified Ju 52ce for Lloyd Aero Boliviano.

Ju 52-3m, works number 4010, No. 621 of the Columbian airforce.

The three Ju-3m's, works numbers 4010-4012, of the Columbian airforce on the Rio Maddalena.

29

Right: **The outer engines of the Colombian Ju 52-3m's were subsequently fitted with Townend rings.**

Centre: **Ju 51-3mce, works number 4013, was the first Ju 52 built as a three-engine machine; it was flown by Lufthansa.**

Bottom: **Works number 4014 was built as Ju 52-3mci for the Finnish company Aero O/Y.**

D-2202 was the first Ju 52-3m fes, works number 4015; it was supplied to Lufthansa and given the name *Richthofen*.

Works number 4016 was a Ju 52-3mba with Hispano-Suiza engines, which was built for the President of the Fédération Aeronautique International (FAI), Prince Bibesco.

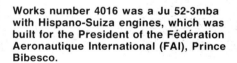

Works number 4017 went, as SE-ADR, to the Swedish AB Aerotransport and was similar to works number 4014.

Works number 4019 went to Lufthansa and was registered as D-2468.

The next works number, 4020, went to Lufthansa and was named after Flight Captain Gustav Dörr, who died on 11 December 1928 in an accident involving Junkers G 31, D-1473 *Rheinland.*

Cabin of a Lufthansa Ju 52-3m.

In those days passengers had more space than in a modern jet.

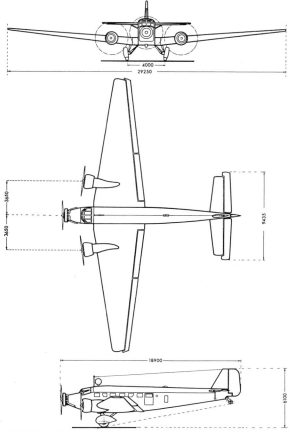

Flächeninhalt des Tragflügels 110,5 m²

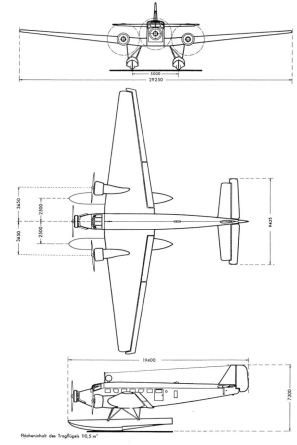

Flächeninhalt des Tragflügels 110,5 m²

Left: **Works drawing of the Ju 52-3ge.**

Works drawing of the Junkers Ju 52-3mW.

33

The road towards large-scale production

In 1931/32 the Reichswehr was increasingly active in preparing the development of the so-called Peacetime Luftwaffe. In March 1932 Inspektion 1 of Reichswehrministerium submitted a report on the capacities of the German aircraft industry. As far as bombers were concerned the position was desperate, only Dornier and Junkers being capable of building such machines. Dornier had built the four-engine Do P and the two-engine Do F (Do II), but now found itself in financial difficulties. In the opinion of Inspektion 1 Junkers had not yet produced any useful military aircraft. The machines built by AB Flygindustri had not taken into account the military requirements of the Reichswehrministerium. The financial position of the company was well-nigh hopeless, while monitoring by Reichs-Verkehrsministerium, Abt. Luftfahrt (the Aviation Dept. of the Transport Ministry), was inadequate. The company was near bankruptcy and was to be put back on its feet with the help of state funds.

The 'Flieger-A-Programm' dated 19 May 1930 had stipulated the establishment of three night bomber squadrons. It proposed that between 1933 and 1937 each general command of the army was to be supported by one night bomber group, each with three squadrons, and from 1938 the army command was to have at its disposal a total of 14 groups with 378 aircraft and 126 reserve aircraft. It was still not decided who was to build these aircraft. Although Inspektion 1 rejected the Junkers aircraft, it was decided on 11 November 1932, in plans for the development of the Luftwaffe, that seven Junkers G 24he night bombers and two Dornier DO 11 night bombers were to be built each month. In other words, at that time no mention was made of the Ju 52, which was then already in production. When Hitler assumed power on 30 January 1933 the situation changed fundamentally. The appoint-ment of Göring as Reichskommissar für Luftfahrt gave the first indication that a new German airforce was to be established at an early date. The Ju 52 was to play an important part.

On 10 April 1933 the Chief of Army Command signed the instruction TA No. 254/33 geh. Kdos. 12IIIB 'Preparation for the establishment of a peace-time airforce'. Under its stipulations three bomber squadrons were to be established by 1 October 1934. Bombergeschwader 1 (Bomber Group 1) with its staff and three squadrons was to be located at Nürnberg-Fürth. Lufthansa and Junkers were to play an important part in this development.

In order to train bomber personnel by the earliest possible date, especially for urgently needed instrument flying, the so-called 'FL-El-Verkehr' of Deutsche Reichsbahn was established (Flugzeug-Eisenbahn). Under the official designation 'Streckenschule der DLH' the training of bomber crews in blind flying started immediately. In addition to ten Do Fs the Ju 52-3m's, D-ABAT, D-ADIH, D-ADYL, D-AFIR, D-AJUP, D-ANUT, D-APYX, D-AQAM, D-ARES, D-ATOL, D-AVES and D-AVIR were being used. D-ADOM, D-ADYL and D-AFIR were the old Lufthansa machines D-2201, D-2202, and D-2468, for which Lufthansa received new machines. This exchange programme with Lufthansa played an important part in the secret development of the new Luftwaffe. DVS obtained DLH machines for brand new Ju 52-3mge's, which formed the basis of the auxiliary bomber squadron. In addition, 100 old aeroplanes of different types went to DVS, for which Lufthansa once again obtained 25 Ju 52-3m's.

The staff of the new Bombergeschwader 1, which was at the same time the HQ of the auxiliary bomber squadron of Lufthansa, now became an independent civil authority in Berlin with the name Verkehrsinspektion der DLH. The bomber squadrons were to be used on ordinary transport routes for air freight purposes, flying individual planes in two-way traffic. Those aircraft that were not in active service had to be ready for flight at their respective bases, where military equipment was also being stored.

All this was only possible by the large scale production of Ju 52-3m's. In 1934 the JU 52-3mge was developed as a successor to the Ju 52-3mfe. It was distinguished by a number of improvements and was fitted with either BMW or Pratt & Whitney Hornet engines. South Africa recieved the first aircraft with Pratt & Whitney Hornets, these being works numbers 4058 to 4060, which were registered as ZS-AFA, ZS-AFB, and ZS-AFC. The machines took off from Dessau on 29 October 1934. Among their pilots were Flight Captains Polte and Neuenhofen, and the South African Captain Fry. A number of varieties of the Ju 52-3mge were built, differing mainly in their engines; these were BMW 132 A/E, BMW 132 A-3, Pratt & Whitney Hornet SIEG, Pratt & Whitney Wasp S3H1-G, Piaggio PXR, Bristol Pegasus VI, and Jumo 205 C. The latter was only fitted into the two DLH machines D-AJYR and D-AQAR. All DLH Ju 52s were given names; in the beginning these were names of famous First World War pilots, and later of those of DLH pilots that had died while on active service. The fastest series was the Ju 52-3mte with BMW 132 G/L engines each of 720 – 800 hp, of which Lufthansa obtained 17 between 1937 and 1939 and which had a maximum speed of 300 km/h.

An entirely different machine was the Ju 52-3mg3e, the auxiliary bomber. Ernst Zindel reports:

An unusual situation arose in 1933/34 after the National Socialists had come to power and when, during preparations for a German airforce, consultations took place to decide which bomber should be built and/or ordered in large numbers. Although a number of different bomber prototypes had been developed for the Reich, it was found that none were suitable aircraft for series construction. Several years earlier a commission of Heereswaffenamt, which for some time had maintained a secret development and investigation group for military aircraft types, had, after a fact-finding visit to Junkers at Dessau, assessed the JU 52, describing it scathingly as entirely unsuitable as a bomber. It came as some surprise when the newly established Reichs Luftfahrtministerium (RLM) whose boss was the former technical director of Deutsche Lufthansa, Erhard Milch (he too came from Junkers Luftverkehrs AG and had joined DLH after the merger), sudddenly saw the successful JU 52 in a new light and immediately declared it to be a 'makeshift bomber'. Nobody at Junkers had expected such a development, and plans for both the single-engine freight machine and the three-engine passenger machine had been exclusively for their use in peacetime air transport. The JU 52 was in no way suitable for the accommodation and horizontal carriage of even small (50 kg) bombs, since the distance between the wing centre section main cross-members, which traversed the fuselage at a distance apart of about 800 mm, was so small that with the best will in the world even small bombs could not be released horizontally. Horizontal release, however, was regarded as vital for the accurate aiming of bombs. In this respect the negative judgement of the Heereswaffenamt was quite understandable; on the other hand we, at Junkers, had never for one minute considered the possibilty of using the Ju 52 for military purposes. When, after the war, East German newspapers stated that the Ju 52 was from the outset, intended as a military 'terror bomber' this was an unfounded and nonsensical invention.

Since the Luftwaffe wanted to start series production of bombers at an early date but had no other suitable model at its disposal, a vertical release mechanism, and consequently the vertical release of bombs, was chosen as a way out; this solution resulted in impaired aiming accuracy. As a result, Heerswaffenamt and Reichsluftfahrtministerium concentrated on the speedy development and testing of vertical bomb racks, which were able to hold either one 250 kg bomb or four 50 kg bombs. Two vertical bomb racks fitted exactly between two main cross-members and the bombs could be released so as to fall between the gaps. Between the three main supports a maximum of eight bomb racks for eight bombs of 250 kg or 32 bombs of 50 kg could be fitted.

The protective armament of the machine consisted of a gunner's station at the top of the fuselage and a lower station in a turret, which served at the same time as observation point for the bombardier. In 1934 Junkers Flugzeugwerk obtained an order from RLM for the accelerated construction of a large number of such bombers; the number of aircraft involved, namely 1200, was altogether unusual for those days and the number of planes to be delivered each month was, after the initial period, in the order of 60.

This RLM order presented Junkers Flugeugwerk with an entirely new situation from the point of view of both production management and organization. The works management, which at the time consisted of Professor Junkers' second son, Claus, as well as the works manager, Oberingenieur Thiedemann, and the head of works preparation, engineer Kuhnen, soon recognized that this tremendous output could only be achieved with an entirely new production method and thoroughly organized production scheduling, in other words by exact planning and execution of the construction processes. By establishing a cycle, similar to a conveyor belt, for the basic construction and end assembly, during which, at each stage, certain synchronized work stages had to be completed, an organized sequence of construction stages was ensured which had to be achieved. The components required for each stage of the cycle had to be delivered on time, and it was even possible to plan variations for different types of machine by exact scheduling. Similarly, exactly planned production and the time-controlled supply of components and units ensured that the requirements of each cycle were met at all stages. In order to prevent too many operating stages from being incorporated in the individual section of the cycle and to prevent individual construction processes and groups from interfering with each other, the aircraft was subdivided into several main units, for example fuselage and wings, which had to be prefabricated and assembled as far as possible and were then finally put together on the assembly lines.

In order to facilitate and simplify these assembly processes as far as possible, the necessary conditions had to be created by relevant construction processes; in addition, special jigs had to be established so that the units were dimensionally accurate. By the preparation and execution of parts and sub-units through the detailed planning of all stages and the introduction of the construction cycle, Junkers created, for the first time in Germany, the facilities for mass-production of large aircraft; this became later the pattern for the entire large-scale aircraft production in Germany. In the USA Ford had already mastered mass-production during the 1920s, where in 1928 as many as 3000 motor cars a day were produced on a total of 15 conveyor belts. In 1957 we saw the same method used when we visited the Lockheed works.

The starting point of this, for that time, gigantic aircraft construction programme was the aircraft acquisition programme of 1 July 1934 according to which 4021 aircraft had to be supplied to the new Luftwaffe by 30 September 1935, among them 450 Ju 52-3mg3e's. By the beginning of 1935 193 machines of this type had been delivered to Tutow, Fassberg, Lechfeld and Prenzlau. The Dornier Do II on the other hand, gave cause for concern. On 19 December 1934 a meeting took place between the later Generals

Sperrle and Keller and the head of LC to discuss the weaknessess of the DO II. The improved types Do 13 and Do 23 were still the subject of continuous complaints on the part of the crews. All parties concerned were aware of the fact that none of the bomber aircraft available at the time, including the Ju 52-3mg3e, met all requirements. But whilst the new types, the Ju 86, Do 17, and He 111, were unavailable, one had to cope with what was available. Major Wolfram von Richtofen, Dr. Ing. and head of the development department of the technical office in the still secret Luftwaffe said in his 'Development Principles' published in August 1934: 'an available machine with limited use is better than no machine ... for each application equipment must be designed and be made available, even if such equipment is initially no more than an intermediate solution or a makeshift solution ... the best and most perfect equipment is useless if its development is not complete.'

When secrecy was lifted in March 1935 the bomber groups 152, 153, 154 and 155 were in existence, and their squadrons distributed over the airfields of Greifswald, Merseburg, Finster-walde, Gotha Giebelstadt, Tutow and Fassberg. Their equipment, which consisted of Do 23s and Ju 52-3mg3e's formed part of the review at the Nazi Party Rally held that year. At the same time other companies started building the Ju 52. This had become necessary since it had become apparent that the parent company would have to start with the large scale production of second generation bombers. During the same year the Ju 52 was to prove itself in active service for the first time.

Ju 52-3m with markings of FL-EI-Verkehr with Reichswehr pilots. On the left the later night fighter pilot Rolf Bassmann of NJG 2.

Ju 52-3mfe, works number 4057, of South African Airways.

Start of large scale production: here showing the construction of fuselages at Dessau.

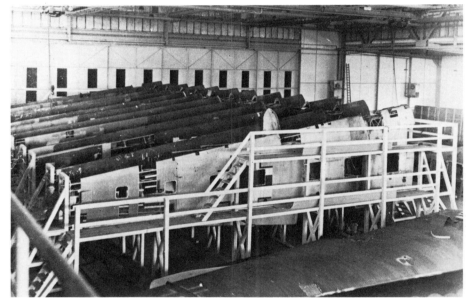

Wing construction at Weserflug. Nordenham.

This unfinished fuselage shows the rugged construction of the Ju 52.

38

Left: **Fuselage interfaces.**

Centre: **Ju 52-3m D-2600, works number 4021 used by Hitler, was given the name** *Immelmann*; **it became later D-AHUT** *H.J. Buddecke.*

Bottom: **The Ju 52-3m dominated German air transport. Here at Berlin-Tempelhof can be seen D-3051, works number 4037 (later D-AMAM) and D-3127, works number 4040 (later D-APAR).**

The conversion of JU 52-3m's for use as auxiliary bombers was mainly carried out by Weserflug. Shown here is the assembly workshop at the Einswarden works.

Bomb bay of Ju 52-3mg3e (Elvemag).

Bomb release hatch.

View of the cockpit.

Bomb release mechanism.

The ventral bomb-aimer's station-cum-lower gun turret.

Ju 52 built at Nordenham had to be taken by boat to Einswarden for flight tests.

Right: **Alfred Keller, Commander of the new KG154, with his officers at Fassberg in 1935.**

Middle: **Ju 52-3mg3e of KG152 during its flights to the Reichsparteitag (Nazi Party Rally) in Nürnberg.**

Bottom: **Austria, too, acquired auxiliary bombers – numbers 36 and 37 – and also OE-HKA a machine for staff flights.**

Works drawing of the Ju 52-3m g3e for use as bomber.

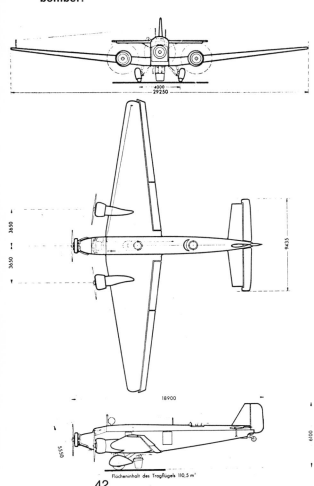

42

Civil war in Spain

On 26 July 1936 Hitler received a delegation sent by General Franco to ask for aircraft for the transportation of Spanish army units stationed in Morocco to Spain, where they were needed to support weak anti-Republican units in certain parts of the country. Hitler immediately promised to send 20 Ju 52-3m transport planes. The first machines took off next day from Berlin-Tempelhof. In order to disguise this operation HISMA was set up, an acronym for Hispano-Marokkanische Transport AG Tetuan-Sevilla. Some personnel were provided by Lufthansa, and the operaton was commanded by Oberleutnant Rudolf Freiherr von Moreau. In all, 86 Luftwaffe volunteers assembled at Doberitz, and on 31 July 1936 the Secretary of State of the Luftwaffe sent them, on their way with the words: 'I am sure you will manage this thing'. In the meantime Sonderstab 'W', a special unit headed by Generalleutnant Wilberg, had been set up in Berlin with the task of arranging all personnel and equipment supplies for the German transport outfit. When the volunteers arrived in Seville they met the Lufthansa captain, Henke. He had been seconded at Las Palmas on his flight back on the trans-oceanic route with his Ju 52 and had gone on to Tetuan. Henke flew Franco's delegation to Germany. He then returned to Spain and formed, with nine other machines, the core of the transport unit, the machines being stationed at Tablada airfield.

The first mission concerned the Spanish foreign legion of General Milan Astrey at Tetuan. No navigation documents were available. Moreau remarked: 'Maps don't exist; I have made a few calculations on a piece of paper about routes and flight times to Tetuan; apart from that follow me and land where I land!' The Republicans soon realized what was afoot when Ju 52s constantly crossed the Straits of Gibraltar from Morocco. The air transport crews reported that what seemed like every Republican warship had converged in the Straits of Gibraltar and fired at every passing Ju 52. The battle cruiser *Jaime I,* in particular, was fitted with well functioning anti-aircraft artillery as well as turrets equipped with 31.5 cm guns that reached as far as Tetuan airport. Since Franco had neither naval forces nor bomber aircraft, there was no possibility of driving *Jaime I* away. Moreau saw that the only way of eliminating *Jaime I* was an air attack, and two Ju 52s, fitted with vertical bomb magazines (Elvemag), were equipped accordingly. Specialized equipment for loading the SC250 bombs was not available; they had to be placed into the magazines by hand. Moreau himself and his radio operator flew one of the machines, Flugkapitän Henke and Leutnant Graf Hoyos the other. On 13 August, at 0400 hours, they took off from Tablada. Moreau was unsuccessful, but Henke and Joyos managed two hits from a height of 500 m. The Republicans announced: 'Great losses, several hundred dead, vessel disabled and towed to Cartagena'. From then on the air transport operations were carried out without interference. By transporting around 15000 Moroccan soldiers and legionnaires, the foundations were laid for Franco's success. After the completion of their transport tasks all Ju 52s of the Moreau squadron were modified as bombers. They formed the nucleus of the combat group K88, formed in November 1936 after the arrival of the main contingent of the actual Condor Legion, which consisted of Moreau's squadron and three additional Ju 52-3mg3e squadrons.

The transfer of this group from Stettin and Swinemünde had been carried out under the code name 'Winterübung Rügen'. Subsequently Moreau established the first Spanish national bomber squadron, based on ten German Ju 52s with Spanish crews. This squadron was stationed at Salamanca. From here, Moreau succeeeded in supplying from the air by low flying aircraft forces trapped in the Alcazar at Toledo. Moreau managed three flights, after which his Ju 52 was so badly damaged that the supply flights had to be discontinued. Meanwhile, the Luftwaffe had recognized that the Spanish operations provided useful experience in air combat and sent the then inspector of bomber pilots, Oberst Pflugbeil, to Seville in order to assist in the establishment of the bomber squadron. His code name, 'Paul', was translated into Spanish and the first machines of Moreau's squadron were given the name 'Pablo'. Three further planes came from Germany, and they were given the name 'Pedro'. Work of the 'Pedros y Pablos' started at the Talavera front, when the enemy positions were softened up by bombs. The aircraft were subsequently used in a number of different combat areas. During the course of an attack on Bilbao they were, for the first time, subjected to intensive anti-aircraft fire. It is worth mentioning that at this time the members of the squadron flew in civilian clothes, since the deployment of this German unit was meant to be secret. On 4 November 1936 a Ju 52, piloted by Leutnant Kolbitz, was the first to be shot down by one of the increasingly large number of Soviet-made fighter planes in the area of Madrid. On 15 November an air combat took place between Moreau's squadron and about 25 Polikarpov I-15s over Madrid. As a result the slower Ju 52 had to be withdrawn rapidly from Spain and replaced by more modern bombers.

Early in 1937 a test combat squadron was set up consisting of three each of the He IIIB, Do 17E and Ju 86D. As early as April 1937 the entire K88 combat group was equipped with He IIIB2s. The Ju 52 was only used as transport plane with a supply function between Germany and Spain. Construction of the 'makeshift bomber', the Ju 52-3mg3e, ceased, while construction of the transport variant continued, and this now became the standard transport plane for the Luftwaffe, built on a large scale by Weserflug and ATG. The last 14 Ju 52-3mg3e's of K88 remained with the air forces of General Franco.

It is a little known fact that the Ju 52 was also used by the Communists in Spain. As early as 11 August 1936 a Ju 52 of Moreau's unit had to land near Azuaga in the Badajos Province, then still in the hands of the Republicans. On board were its German crew and a Spaniard. Since the machine had German markings it was returned to Germany in order to avoid diplomatic complications. Soon afterwards one of the Ju 52s handed over to Franco's air force and piloted by the Spaniard Ananias Sanjuan landed at the airport of Cuatro Vientos near Madrid. The pilot handed the machine over to the Republicans. A second Franco Ju 52 crew also changed sides to the Republicans and landed near Alcocer in the Province of Guadalajara. These two, now Republican, Ju 52s were used for transport operations, mainly in the south of Spain, the reason being that the Ju 52 was known as a Franco aircraft and was therefore attacked by Communist Spanish fighter aircraft and anti-aircraft units. One of these two Ju 52s was lost in an accident, when a Communist Spanish fighter pilot, by the name of Torras, collided with the Ju 52 when landing at Figueras and was killed. Nothing is known about the fate of the other Ju 52.

Start of troop transports from Morocco to Spain. The Ju 52 in the foreground still has the German registration number D-ATRN.

Troops in Morocco patiently waiting for their flight.

Transport under very primitive conditions.

45

The Ju 52 normally had to be cleaned after each flight. The Moroccans were bad air travellers!

Battle cruiser *Jaime I*. The bomb damage to the forward end of the ship is clearly visible.

The uniform in which Leutnant Max Graf Hoyos bombed *Jaime I* with a Ju 52, flown by Flight Captain Henke (right).

46

Ju 52-3mg3e coming in to land in Mallorca, 1936.

Ju 52-3mg3e of Franco's airforce landing at its point of deployment, 1937.

In 1937 an Italian Romeo Ro 37 rammed a Ju 52-3mg3e belonging to one of Franco's air squadrons, which had been given the name *Navarra*.

As early as the Spanish Civil War the Ju 52 was also used for transporting wounded soldiers.

Ju 52-3mg3e of 3/K88 during a bombing raid. The squadron markings were later also used by III/KG53 of the Luftwaffe.

General Moscardo, the defender of the Alcazar in Toledo, greets Major Nielsen of the Condor Legion. Behind him is Generalmajor von Richthofen.

48

Visit of the last commander-in-chief of the Condor Legion, Generalmajor von Richthofen, to General Moscardo. From right to left: von Richthofen, Moscardo and Major Nielsen.

Moving a unit of the Condor Legion by Ju 52-3mg3e.

Civil aviation between Germany and Spain continued despite the civil war.

49

One of the two Ju 52s which had been hijacked by Spanish pilots and flown to the Republican lines, where they were used by the airforce.

Command post of the Condor Legion in 1938, with Colonel Troncoso of the *Navarra* Brigade; Oberst Seidemann, Chief-of-Staff, Condor Legion.

50

Ju 52 – development before the Second World War

Exports of the Ju 52-3m as a transport plane continued to increase. The main buyers were the Swedish AB Aerotransport, who ordered another six machines, and South African Airways who had a futher eleven. The Swedes, however, insisted on modification of the Ju 52's basic concepts; in particular the head of the technical bureau of AB Aerotransport (ABA), K.H. Larson, requested a fundamental modificaton of engine installation. He reported:

'I suggested Pratt & Whitney Wasp S3H-1-G engines each of 550 hp, with a reduction of 3:2 and a variable pitch three-blade constant-speed propeller to be made by Hamilton. The engines were to be given NACA cowls in order to improve cooling and maintain a waste-gas-heated air intake aimed at reducing carburettor icing – all problems which we had experienced with SE-ADR. I also requested that the thrust line of the outer engines should be aligned with the longitudinal axis of the aircraft. Variable pitch propellers made it possible, at a height of 3000 m, to fly with full power and achieve a cruising speed of 250 km/h, with the noise level inside the cabin remaining very low. We were therefore able to fly non-stop on the Stockholm-Berlin route (800 km) and the Copenhagen-Amsterdam route (633 km) both economically and success-fully. This version of the Ju 52-3m (Ju 52-3mL) was equipped with the most modern American instruments, among them an artificial horizon by Sperry, a gyro compass and a precision altimeter made by Koolsman. In order to make the passenger cabin more attractive we consul-ted Professor Sune Lindström, who designed new chairs and who was responsible both for the materials used and the interior fittings. A futher improvement was the streamlined design of the wheels which permitted higher cruising speeds.'

The modifications requested by ABA resulted in an increased speed of travel, from 170 to 220 km/h. South African Airways, having learnt of the ABA modifications, ordered the same type.

Of the six Ju 52-3mL's subsequently ordered the modifications requested by ABA had not been carried out on SE-AER and SE-AES. On 9 April 1940, when the invasion of Norway and Denmark started, SE-AER was at Oslo-Fornebu. Both machines were sold to British Airways in 1945. At about the same time Austria had bought 12 Ju 52-3m's. Nine flew for Osterreichische Luftverkehrs-AG (OLAG), one was used for VIP transport purposes by the Austrian air force, and two were auxiliary bombers of the Ju 52-3mg3e version.

On 11 March 1938, Hitler had ordered prepara-tions to commence for 'Fall Otto' the military occupation of Austria. The operation was headed by Generalmajor Wolff, of Luftkreis V, who was the first to land on 12 March 1938, in a Ju 52 at Vienna Aspern. The operations by the German army had met with Austrian resistance and had been unable to proceed. As a result Wolff mobilized Lehrgeschwader 1, Tutow, a training group, and proceeded to fly to Vienna. It has been impossible to ascertain, whether at this time the Luftwaffe budget contained transport units. It is certain, however, that some transport aircraft of the Luftwaffe were used on this occasion. As a result of this operation the Ju 52s sold by Germany to Austria 'returned to the Fatherland', to use the words of German propa-ganda of that time.

At the same time preparations were under way in case military conflict with Czechoslovakia should occur; these were given the cover name 'Fall Grün'. 'Planstudie Grün', issued by the commanding general of Luftwaffengruppe 1 on

11 July 1938, formed the basis of operations by the Luftwaffe. In case of military resistance the 7th Luft-Division in conjunction with the combat groups zbV1, 2, 4, 5 and 6 as well as two paratrooper battalions and two airborne units were to play a decisive role. These units were put on alert in Upper Silesia in September 1938. Even though no active service was required, since the Czech government ceded the Sudetenland to Germany without resistance, the operation was carried out in the form of an exercise and resulted in experience gained in the use of paratroopers and airborne units.

In 'Fall Grün' transport units were for the first time mentioned under the name 'Kampfgruppe zur besonderen Verwendung (KGr zbV)'. In effect they had been in existence since October 1937, when KGr zbV1 was formed from IV/KG152 'Hindenburg'. This was strengthened and subsequently divided, so that from 1 August 1938 KGr zbV1 and 2 were in existence. All further KGr zbVs were formed on an *ad hoc* basis from training schools and reserve units, disbanded after the conclusion of the specific operation for which they had been required, and returned to their base units. The KGr zbV disappeared after the formation of transport groups 'Transportgeschwader' (TG), in May 1943. The tactical unit remained in existence, however, in the form of a group consisting of a flight and 4-5 squadrons, each consisting of 12 Ju 52s. A further special unit equipped with Ju 52s was the so-called 'Regierungsstaffel', which was formed in January 1938 and consisted of VIP transport aircraft for generals and prominent party members. The following were made available:

D-ARET *Kurt Schuhmann*
Reichsminister Rudolf Hess
D-AFAM *Max von Müller*
Reichminister Dr. Goebbels
D-APPA *Otto Kissenbert*
Reichsführer SS Heinrich Himmler
D-AJIM *Hermann Göring*
Gen. Feldmarschall von Blomberg

D-ATUF *Graf Schlieffen*
Generaloberst von Fritsch
D-AYHO *Peter Strasser*
Generaladmiral Raeder
A-AZIS *Horst Wessel*
SA-Stabschef Lutze
D-AQUIT *Major Dincklage*
Reichsleiter Robert Ley
D-AMYY *Wilhelm Siegert*
Ambassador von Ribbentrop
D-ANAO *Joachim von Schröder*
Reserve Aircraft

To these were added D-2600 *Immelmann,* Hitler's aircraft, and D-2527, Göring's *Manfred von Richthofen'* which had been painted red. During the course of the next few years these Ju 52s were replaced by Focke-Wulf Fw 200 and returned to the DLH fleet with different markings.

Despite its involvement with the Luftwaffe, Lufthansa never lost sight of its aim of worldwide air transport. One of the most important targets in this direction was the establishment of a route to the Far East, bypassing the USSR. As early as 1934 Flugkapitän Untucht had completed a long-distance flight from Berlin to Shanghai in a Ju 52. In 1936 the technical director of Lufthansa, Freiherr von Gablenz, prepared an expedition to Afghanistan, whose object was reconnoitring the possibility of flying over the Pamir and Hindu Kush. The Junkers Ju 52-3m D-AVUP under Flugkapitän Drechsel, accompanied by Afghan air force officers, completed the first flight from Kabul across the Pamir at heights of up to 4000-5000 m and returned to Kabul once it had reached Chinese territory. The foundation for a futher advance had thus been laid. On 14 August 1937 the Ju 52-3m D-ANOY *Rudolf von Thüna* under Freiherr von Gablenz, accompanied by Flugkapitän Untucht and Oberfunkermaschinist Karl Kirchhoff, took off from Tempelhof. A second machine, D-AMIP, was to follow one week later under Flugkapitän Drechsel. The flight as far as Kabul presented no major problems. The first attempt

52

to cross the Pamir produced, however, difficulties with the variable-pitch propellers. On 24 August the narrow Wakhan Pass was negotiated and after passing over Chotan the aircraft landed at Ansi. On its return flight from the turning point of Su-Chow in China, D-ANOY had to carry out an emergency landing at Chotan and was held there by rebels for four weeks. During this period the machine was left outside without any cover. A search expedition had been started from Germany, and this was discontinued since Gablenz and his people succeeded in getting D-ANOY ready for take-off. Although the aircraft was low on fuel and oil it succeeded in reaching Kabul, where it was met by the two search planes Ju 52 D-AEHE and D-AOLO. The flight captains Graf Castell and von Gössel greeted von Gablenz and his people with great relief. A third Ju 52, D-AXAT, under Flugkapitän Kuring also arrived in Kabul. Gablenz returned, with Untucht and Kirchhoff, to Berlin in D-AEHE.

Even the British, who were proud of the achievements of their aircraft industry, were unable to resist the quality of the German Ju 52-3m. In January 1937 British Airways Limited started a freight service with two Ju 52-3m's, G-AERU *Juno* and G-AERX *Jupiter*, which had been bought from the Swedish AB Aerotransport as SE-AER and SE-AES. A third machine, G-AFAP *Jason* was bought direct from Junkers. All three were stationed at Gatwick and flew cargo to Hanover and Stockholm until the outbreak of the war. After that they flew once weekly from Perth to Stavanger, Oslo, Stockholm, and Helsinki until German forces occupied Norway on 9 April 1940, when *Jason* fell into German hands in Oslo while *Juno* managed to find its way back from Stockholm to Gatwick. *Jupiter* was moved to Africa in 1940 and flew from November 1940 onward for BOAC on the Takoradi-Khartoum route. *Juno* was used for spare parts. In September 1941 *Jupiter* and *Juno* (after repair work) went to the Belgian airline Sabena and were used in the Belgian Congo. In

1939 a Polish Ju 52, SP-AKX, had escaped from Poland to Britain; it was used by BOAC as G-AGAE. The change of aircraft markings entailed dificulties, so that the Air Ministry withdrew the machine. Only after 1945 were Ju 52s to fly once again for a British airline.

Since the production of second generation bombers had by then started, the production of the Ju 52 was now entirely geared to transports. Special versions were only built in small numbers, while large-scale production was carried out by ATG in Leipzig and at the IFA works (Junkers). As early as 1937 prototype aircraft of a new version, g4e, had been built and subsequently production changed smoothly from g3e to g4e. This version had the same BMW 132A engines, of 660 hp each. The loading bay had been fitted with a reinforced floor, and large loading hatches on the right-hand side of the fuselage as well as on the roof of the cabin. In order to secure the loads, steel pipe lashing frames had been attached to the side walls of the loading area. Starting with works number 6049 the landing gear had been reinforced, so as to be suitable for a take-off weight of 10,500 kg. Most of the Ju 52-3mg4e's were built as military transport planes, although Lufthansa also received about a dozen of these machines. Three planes went to the Swiss military administration. These machines still exist to-day. Their landing gear could not be exhanged for floats. The machine gun support structure at the back of the fuselage was modified so that it took an MG131 instead of the MG15. Only a small number of models suitable for parachuting still had the MG turret of the g3e bombers.

In addition to transport units, communications units also received a number of Ju 52-3m's. After the 'Sudeten Crisis' KGr zbV2, 4, 5 and 6 were disbanded, leaving only KG zbV1 and the staff of KG zbV2. Having been let down by France and England, Czechoslovakia was invaded by Germany on 15 March 1939. This was to have an unpleasant aftermath for France in 1940. Germany now held all Czech fortifications, and these were used by German paratroopers to practise the conquest of strong fortifications. The conqueror of Eben Emael in 1940, Leutnant Witzig, said after the war: 'We would never have been able to crack the Czech fortifications. Eben Emael on the other hand was child's play'. In June 1939 the exercise 'Generalstabsreise 1939' took place over a number of days; it concentrated entirely on the use of the Luftwaffe against Poland. This exercise used, for the first time, 'Fliegerführer zbV'. Even though the use of the 7th Luft-Division with a transport unit and a paratrooper battalion had been scheduled, the 'Fliegerführer zbV' were still an unknown quantity. Such a unit had existed under the last head of the Condor Legion, Generalmajor von Richthofen, and his chief of staff Oberstleutnant Seidmann. In 1939 the German air transport units consisted entirely of the task forces KGr zbV1 and 2 with a total of eight squadrons, each consisting of 12 Ju 52s. This would mean that only 96 – 100 transport aircraft were available. On the other hand a report by the chief of general staff of the Luftwaffe (Gen. Qu. 6. Abt.) of 2 September 1939 registers a total of 552 Ju 52s. This means that around 450 Ju 52s were available at the various flying schools for immediate action.

Ju 52-3m, works number 5633, which had, at the request of AB Aerotransport, all three engines fitted so that their longitudinal axes were parallel.

Ju 52-3mge works number 4076, became D-AJAT in 1939; it went to Spain in May 1938 as M-CABC of Iberia; later EC-AAK, it was in service until 1948.

54

Ju 52-3mg3e, No. 36 of the Austrian air force. It joined the German Luftwaffe in 1938 after modification work by Weserflug.

D-ALYL, ex-OE-LAR, works number 5180, joined the Luftwaffe in 1939 as NG+VY, later 1Z+RV.

Start of a flight of a Ju 52-3mge of Deruluft from Berlin-Tempelhof to Moscow.

55

Ju 52-3mge, works number 6360, at the Buda-Ö airport.

Another Hungarian Ju 52 was rammed at Vienna-Aspen by a Bf 109B-2 of the Luftwaffe in 1938.

Ju 52-3mge of Eurasia in Mongolia.

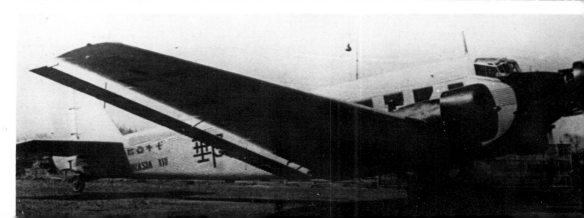

Ju 52-3m *Nampula* **CR-AAL,
works number 5973, of Deta-
Mozambique.**

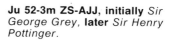

Ju 52-3m **ZS-AJJ, initially** *Sir
George Grey,* **later** *Sir Henry
Pottinger.*

Ju 52-3m **works number
4064, I-BIZI, used as a military transport during the
war.**

57

Ju 52-3m PP-CAY *Marimba*, **works number 4042, of Syndicato Condor, Brazil; previously D-3136 of Lufthansa.**

Ju 52-3m OO-AGW, works number 5672, of the Belgian airline.

Ju 52-3m D-AGST *Maipo* , works number 5261, became PP-CAZ of Syndicato Condor.

Lufthansa carried out regular airmail flights to South Africa routing via Seville and Bathurst, West Africa. The illustration shows the Ju 52 at Bathurst.

Ju 52-3mte D-ANOY *Rudolf von Thüna* works number 5663, flew across the Pamir.

Von Gablenz, Flugkapitän Untucht (right) and wireless operator Kirchoff in Berlin after their flight across the Pamir.

A typical view of
Tempelhof airport,
around 1936. Ju 52s
dominated Germany's
air transport.

Ju 52-3mho, D-AQAR
Walter Höhndorf
works number 4055,
with Junkers diesel
engines.

Crash of Ju 52-
3mg3e, 33 + K39,
works number 5462
on 6 April 1937 near
Liegnitz. The pilot,
Obergefreiter Feld-
kirchner, lost his life.

Ju 52-3mge of the Danish
airline with neutrality markings, which were used from
the beginning of the war
until the occupation of
Denmark in 1940.

Ju 52-3mreo D-AWBR in
1938 in India.

Ju 52-3m LN-DAH, works
number 5489 of the Norwe-
gian Det Norske Luftfahrt-
selskab.

61

Ju 52-3mfe D-ASIS
Wilhelm Cuno, **works number 4074, of Deutsche Lufthansa.**

Ju 52-3mfe D-3131 *Werner Voss,* **works number 4041, became D-ARAM in 1935.**

Ju 52-3mge D-ALAN
Eduard Dostler, **works number 5010, after a crash-landing at Munich – Oberwiesenfeld on 22 October 1937 at 2230 hours as a result of faulty landing gear.**

62

Göring used three Ju 52s, painted red, as personal planes, all were named *Manfred von Richtofen*. **The illustration shows D-2527, works number 4022, later D-AGUK.**

Manfred von Richtofen **No. 2 D-ABAQ, works number 4066.**

Manfred von Richthofen **No. 3 D-ABIK, works number 4069.**

63.

Left: **Prominent Nazis also enjoyed flying in the Ju 52. Here is the brown D-AZIZ** *Horst Wessel* **of SA chief-of-staff Lutze. 105**

Right: **The then Reichskriegsminister Generalfeldmarschall von Blomberg had at his disposal a Ju 52-3m D-AJIM** *Hermann Göring,* **works number 4050.**

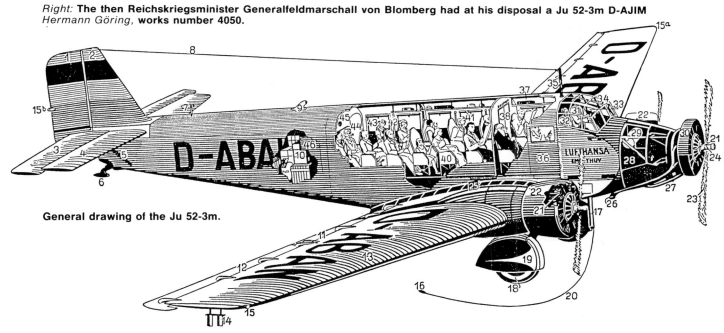

General drawing of the Ju 52-3m.

1. Rudder	13. Wing	23. Twin-bladed propeller	35. Mast for fixed antenna
2. Tail fin	14. Landing lights	24. Propeller hub	36. Cabin door
3. Elevator	15. Starboard navigation light	25. Fuel vent dome	37. Smokers' compartment
4. Horizontal stabilizer	15a. Port side navigation light	26. Central engine exhaust pipe	38. Sliding door
5. Strut for horizontal stabilizer	15b. Tail light	27. Cabin warm air heating pipe	39. Luggage compartments
6. Tail skid	16. Effective area of antenna	28. Engine mounting	40. Seat, adjustable
7. Vent for remote-reading compass	17. Antenna conduit	29. Oil tank	41. Roller blinds
8. Fixed antenna	18. Main wheel	30. Townend ring (central engine)	42. Individual fresh air hoses
9. Fresh air inlet	19. Wheel spat	31. Pilot	43. Boarding hatch
10. Freight compartment	20. Trailing antenna	32. Radio operator	44. Lavatory door
11. Starboard flap	21. Air cooled radial engine, 650 hp	33. Control wheel	45. Altimeter
12. Starboard aileron	22. Engine cowl, NACA type	34. Cockpit (closed)	46. Freight compartment door

Ju 52s in Poland and Norway 1939 – 1940

The attack on Poland took place under the code name 'Fall Weiss', the operational plan which stipulated Luftflotten 1 and 4 as the assault units. The transport and landing units were under the direct command of the Supreme Commander of the Luftwaffe (ObdL). They included the staff of the 7th Flieger-Division under Generalmajor Student, who was stationed at Hirschberg, Silesia, as well as KGr zbV1 and 2, KGr zbV172 and Fallschirmjäger-Regiment 1 (1st Paratrooper Regiment). The attack started on 1 September 1939 at 0445 hours. After one Polish army after the other had capitulated, the Polish capital Warsaw, which had been surrounded on 19 September, was requested to capitulate, but was refused. After the return of the German negotiator a dozen He 111 of I/KG4 flew over Warsaw, dropping large numbers of propaganda leaflets in which the population was requested to leave Warsaw within twelve hours in an easterly direction, since, should the Polish commander-in-chief refuse to capitulate, the city would be bombed from the air. Further leaflets were dropped on 18, 19, 22, and 24 September. The Poles refused to surrender. About 100,000 Polish soldiers barricaded themselves in various parts of the city and prepared for street fighting. Geralmajor von Richthofen, the 'Fliegerführer zbV' received the order to carry out the bombardment. He had at his disposal 240 Ju 87, Stuka, dive bombers but these were unsuitable for dropping incendiary bombs. Since all bomber units had been withdrawn from Poland, his only option was to load Ju 52 transporters with incendiary bombs and to throw these from their crates through the lateral hatches. This operation started on 24 September. On 25 September Richthofen's units released 72 tonnes of incendiary bombs and 486 tonnes of high-explosive bombs over Warsaw. If one assumes that the incendiary bombs have an average weight of 2 kg this means that 36000 incendiary bombs were dropped on Warsaw. The city capitulated on 28 September 1939.

In October 1939 Hitler issued Directive No. 6 on offensive warfare on the Western Front. This marked the beginning of efforts to establish an operational plan for the Western Front, which was to continue until the spring of 1940. One day later Grossadmiral Raeder, Commander-in-Chief of the Navy, reported to Hitler on the strategic significance Norway had for Germany. On 16 January 1940 preparatory work was started by the Anglo-French general staffs on military action in Scandinavia. Berlin was informed of these activities eleven days later and started preparing operation 'Weserübung', the occupation of Danish and Norwegian bases. On 21 February 1940 General von Falkenhorst was put in charge of 'Weserübung'.

The Luftwaffe part of 'Weserübung' was the responsibility of the 10th Fliegerkorps under Generalleutnant Geissler. A small working team was formed for the airborne operations, headed by the Techincal Director of Lufthansa, Oberstleutnant der Reserve Carl-August Freiherr von Gablenz. It was intended to set up seven transport units, five of which were to be equipped with the Ju 52-3mg3e, one with the Ju 52-3m with an increased range, in other words the same type that had been used by Gablenz when he crossed the Pamir, while one group had at its disposal large Ju 90, Fw 200 transporters, and the old Junkers G 38, D-APIS. On 11 March von Gablenz held a preliminary meeting with all intended group commanders. During the next two days the office of 'Transportchef' was established up at the 10th Fliegerkorps under the command of von Gablenz. This designation was later changed to 'Transport-Chef (Land)' to distinguish it from the relevant naval equivalent. As early as 14 March a preliminary operational order was issued, still for an 'exercise'. Not until 29 March was the final operational order for 'Weserübung' given. On 28 March the United War Council in London decided to lay mines in Norwegian waters on 5 April and to occupy points of military importance in Norway. As early as 31 March, on the other hand, all commanding officers of the units that needed to be transported had been informed by Oberkommando der Wehrmacht (OKW) on all questions connected with the operation, although this was still described as an exercise.

On 4th April von Gablenz's staff had finalized the transport schedule. On 6 April having been given the password 'Elbing', all group commanders of the transport units and the remaining staff members were acquainted with the latest operational orders. The targets of the air landings operation were: Oslo, Stavanger, Aalborg-West, and Aalborg-East. Paratrooper units of Fallschirmjäger-Regiment 1 were to be taken to the operational area by KGr zbV102, 103 and 104. KGr zbV101, 106 and 107, equipped with 293 Ju 52-3mg3e's, were to fly army units and their equipment. KGr zbV105 had 33 Ju 52s, three of which were the standard g3e, the remaining 30 were Ju 52s with increased range. With these were five Ju 90s of Lufthansa, two Fw 200s and the old G 38. KGr zbV1 had been increased to 215 machines and an additional squadron of KGr zbV9. Of these, all were intended for landing place reconnoitring in the areas of Narvik, Trondheim and Oslo. On 8 April the operational order was received. Most of the bases were in North-West Germany, an area under the command of Geralmajor Missfelder. Of these, one was the base at Uetersen, where on 8 April 1940 Generalstabschef der Luftwaffe, Generalleutnant Jeschonnek arrived to supervise the operation. The first to be alerted and instructed were the pilots of the reconnaissance machines for Oslo-Fornebu, Kjeller, Kristiansand, Trondheim and Narvik. The start of 'Weserübung' was fixed for 9 April at 0500 hours.

Flugkapitän Henke of Lufthansa, by then Oberleutnant der Reserve der Luftwaffe, was the first to take off, at 0340 hours. It was he who had bombed *Jaime I* in Spain. Bad weather prevented the punctual start of the transport squadrons; delays arising of up to 45 minutes. Nevertheless, all machines took off eventually. It now became apparent how useful was the blind flying training which had been introduced by von Gablenz as early as 1929 at DLH and which had met, initially, opposition from many pilots, but which had subsequently become compulsory for all transport pilots. Because of the forecast of poor weather conditions some of the transport squadrons left up to 45 minutes late. The machine piloted by Oblt. Matthias, which had been intended for reconnaissance duty in the Trondheim area, was forced by anti-aircraft guns to make an emergency landing. Matthias was subsequently able to assist with improved landing facilities. The landing operations at Aalborg-West and East went according to schedule; nor did any major problems arise at Stavanger. The landing operation at Oslo-Fornebu on the other hand presented major difficulties.

The advance guard of the paratroopers radioed the news that it had to return because of bad weather. As a result, Generalleutnant Geisler ordered all machines to return. This order was not executed, however, by the second group, zbV-Gruppe 103; instead, it succeeded in landing at Fornebu, despite fierce defensive action by the Norwegians, during the course of which their commander, Hauptmann Wagner, was killed. Only part of the following group, zbV 102, was informed of the new arrangement. Meanwhile a German ship stationed outside Oslo harbour sent a radio message that Ju 52s were landing at Fornebu. As a result the chief-of-staff of the 10th Fliegerkorps immediately ordered the take-off of all available machines. Von Gablenz now had the difficult task of ensuring that the build-up of units could proceed so that no overcrowding arose at Oslo airport. In order to prevent German machines from landing, the Norwegians had pushed aircraft onto the runway to set fire to some of them. It was therefore only possible for single planes to land; nevertheless, in addition to the combat units, over 50 transport planes had to land every 150 minutes. Without the personal intervention of Oberstleutnant von Gablenz and the other section leaders and technical staff, Fornebu would probably have ground to a standstill. Great efforts were made to overcome the threatening situation. As a result of aircraft losses through excessive use or enemy action it became necessary during the course of the operation to amalgamate the zbV-Gruppen 101 and 102 as well as 103 and 104 to form the new groups 101 and 104 respectively. The latter was moved to Copenhagen. In Oslo an office was set up for the Transportchef (Land) under the command of Major Beckmann, an old pilot of 1917/18 and later commander of KG zbV500 (Demyansk), which provided transport links to Trondheim. Oberstleutnant von Gablenz was given, at short notice, III/zbV172, zbV11 and 12 as well as zbV9 for transporting anti-aircraft guns and other urgently required equipment. The volume of transported goods was extraordinary for that period, as will be illustrated by the following figures.

By the beginning of May 1940, 36 battalions of infantry and sappers, 12 regimental and divisional headquarters and 10 mountain artillery units complete with all necessary equipment had been transported. In addition, 49 Ju 52 loads were flown for the navy and 177 Ju 52s conveyed radio equipment for the army and air forces. About $1\frac{1}{4}$ million litres of fuel needed by the Luftwaffe, bombs (140 SC250s, 20 SC500s, 1800 SC50s, and 1000 fragmentation bombs weighing 18 kg each) and other equipment for the airport operating units and other ground organizations were moved in the course of about 600 Ju 52 flights. A total of 98 flights took anti-aircraft artillery and ammunition to Norway.

The Narvik missions are a story in themselves. These missions were based partly on Hamburg-Fuhlsbüttel, partly on Oslo. During the flights Oberleutnant Henke, Hauptmann Reichel, Hauptmann Sluzalek and Feldwebel Haumann distinguished themselves particularly. Henke and Sluzalek were experienced Lufthansa flight captains, whilst Henke had become known through his flights with Fw 200 Condors to New York and Tokyo; Sluzalek had been a bomber pilot during 1917/18. Despite the fact that on their supply flights to Narvik the machines were under fire from British warships and were, at times, badly damaged, all missions were completed. On 13 April 1940 a particularly risky operation was carried out. In it, a Ju 52 squadron of zbV-Gruppe 102 under the command of Oberst Baur de Betaz had to land a mountain unit with all its equipment at Narvik. The only landing place was the frozen Lake Hartvig, and it was likely that the machines would be lost; a return flight was not possible for lack of fuel alone. Three further Ju 52s (modified for long range operation) noted on the next day that the mountain unit had been landed. Three of the aircraft, some of which had come from B-Schule Wiener-Neustadt, landed in Sweden as result of a navigational error. They did not return to Germany until 2 September 1940, fitted with Swedish markings.

Whereas the zbV Gruppen 106 and 107, of Luftflotte 5, remained in Norway for urgent transport operations, all other zbV Groups returned to Germany. This completed the task of Oberstleutnant von Gablenz in Norway. The headquarters of Transportchef (Land) ceased its activity. Even though in 1917 an amphibian operation had taken place during the occupation of the island of Ösel by the army and navy with the co-operation of flying units, the action described here was the first sea-air landing exercise in history.

September 1939.
IV/KG zbV2, ready for
operations in Poland.

Machine of the commander of KG zbV2, Major
Beckmann, on 2 September 1939 at Sorau.

Crews of KG zbV2, at
its operational meeting
at Sorau, 9 September
1939.

Waiting for the next operation of
KG zbV2.

Ju 52-3mg4e of KG zbV1 at Uetersen on
9 April 1940 before loading infantry.

At Uetersen 8 April 1940: third from right
Luftwaffe chief-of-staff, Generalleutnant
Jeschonnek; first from right,
Generalmajor Missfelder, commander of
the north-west German airfields.

Infantry embarking for Norway on 9 April 1940.

A Ju 52-3meg4e on its flight back from Norway.

Ju 52s of KGr zbV104 shortly before the Norwegian coast.

70

Above the snow-covered mountains of northern Norway.

Parachutes landing containers with supplies at Narvik.

Infantry landing at Stavanger-Sola.

Ju 52s of KGr zbV105: first
contacts between German and
Norwegian soldiers.

Ju 52-3mg3e of I/KGr zbV172
at Kjevik, early April 1940.

This Ju 52 of KG zbV1 crashed
on 16 April 1940, with 16
soldiers on board, into a lake
near the Flekkefjords.

72

On its flight to Narvik, on 14 April 1940, this Ju 52 accidentally strayed into Sweden and was shot down by Swedish anti-aircraft artillery.

This Ju 52 crash-landed on 14 April 1940 near Mariestad in Sweden and broke through thin ice.

Ju 52 SE+HU, works number 6132, of Flugzeugführerschule B8 Wiener-Neustadt, accidentally strayed on its way to Narvik, onto Swedish territory and landed at Grebbestad on 14 April 1940.

73

Top: **SE + HU returned on 2 September 1940 to Germany bearing Swedish civil markings SE-AKT.**

Right: **SE + KC of KGr zbV102, which had started from Neumünster in a northerly direction on 13 April 1940, like SE + HU strayed into Sweden. It landed on 17 April at Vallsta (Sweden).**

Bottom: **On 2 September SE + KC, works number 6664, also returned to Germany with Swedish markings SE + AKR.**

The third Ju 52 involved in the Narvik operation to land in Sweden as a result of a navigational error was SE + IM which touched down near Grums on 16 April 1940.

SE + IM, too, was partly overpainted in black and given the Swedish markings SE-AKS. Subsequently, on 2 September 1940, the machine was allowed to return to Germany.

The Ju 52, badly mauled in Holland and Belgium 1940

On 1 May 1940 Hitler fixed the beginning of 'Fall Gelb', the German offensive in the West, for 5 May. In Norway heavy fighting continued around Narvik, and a Norwegian government in exile was formed on 5 May in London. German plans, however, were upset by the weather, for on 7 May Hitler had to postpone the beginning of the offensive to 9 May. Although Oberst Oster, chief of the central department of the German 'defence', who had previously told the Dutch military attaché to Berlin the date of the beginning of 'Weserübung', also betrayed the starting date of 'Fall Gelb', the other side showed no reaction. The basic concept of the German offensive plan was based on a break-through of tank units through the Ardennes. At the same time a large-scale attack on Holland and Belgium was to divert attention from the tank operation and lure Anglo-French forces to the north.

The decisive factor for this operation was the conquest of the undamaged bridges across the Maas and of the cornerstone of the Belgian defence lines, the fortress Eben Emael. For this purpose Luftlandetruppe (airborne force) was used for the first time; this force's spiritual father was the former First World War fighter pilot, by now Generalmajor, Kurt Student, who commanded all air landing operations of the Western Campaign. Not only paratroopers were used but also a weapon whose existence had been carefully kept secret: the transport glider. The prerequisite of the deployment of both of these components was a large transport fleet, which consisted exclusively of Ju 52-3m's. Only the g4e version was suitable for towing the gliders, since it was fitted with a tailwheel to which the tow coupling could be attached. The units intended for deployment at Eben Emael and the bridges

across the Albert Canal had, as had already been mentioned, previously been used in the Altvater Mountains in Czechoslovakia against the Czech forces. Oberleutnant Rudolf Witzig, who had been given orders to land with his troops direct on Eben Emael, anticipated colossal problems, but in the event the operation went better than he thought. The Belgian fortifications were far less difficult to conquer than the Czech ones, in whose design experienced officers of the old Austro-Hungarian Army had been involved. In particular the Belgian fortress lacked the overlapping artillery and machine gun fields of fire. All air landing operations were to be carried out by the 7th Flieger-Division, under the command of Generalmajor Student. The following transport units were put at his disposal:

KG zbV1 with four groups under the command of Oberst Fritz Morzik. They were to transport the 7th Flieger-Division and parts of the 22nd Luftlande-Infanterie-Division. It was their task to occupy the bridges near Moerdijk and Dordrecht and the airport Waalhaven/Rotterdam.

KG zbV2 under the command of Oberst Conrad with KGr zbV9, 11, 12 and 172, whose task it was to land the 22nd Luftlande-Infanterie-Division at airports in area of the Hague; the division was then to occupy the seat of government and arrest the Queen of the Netherlands.

'Sturmgruppe Koch' had been allocated a special role. It consisted of the groups:

'Granit' under Oberleutnant Witzig, who had been given orders to land with his men on Eben Emael with DFS 230 transport gliders and eliminate the fortress's armaments. He then had to wait for Pionier-Bataillon 5, which was to reach the fortress by land, to establish contact, and complete the rest of the work.

'Beton' under Leutnant Schacht was to occupy the bridge across the Albert Canal near Vroenhoven.

'Stahl' under Oberleutnant Altmann, was given the same task near Veldwezelt, and 'Eisen' under Leutnant Schachter again the same task near Kanne.

Each of the first two groups had been given eleven Ju 52s towing DFS 230 gliders, while 'Stahl' had nine and 'Eisen' ten. This total of 42 Ju 52s belonged to KG zbV 1. A total of 430 Ju 52s was to be available for the operation as a whole. In fact only 401 JU 52s were available on the date of deployment, so that a further 29 had to be brought in from flying schools. The operational strength of the 7th Flieger-Division amounted to 4000 men to which came a further 14,500 men of the 22nd Luftlande-Infanterie-Division. This meant that the entire operation involved the transporting of 18,500 men complete with all their equipment; an air transport operation of proportions never before attempted. The Ju 52-3m was able to carry 14 paratroopers or 14 to 15 infantrymen; if the men carried heavy arms their numbers would be limited to a maximum of six. It was clear that the 430 Ju 52s available would not be able to move the 18,500 fully equipped men at once, so that a shuttle service spread out over two days had to be arranged.

Unfortunately, operations of the group 'Granit' started with an accident, when, South of Cologne, two Ju 52s nearly collided in mid-air. The pilot of the second Ju 52 of this unit descended steeply to avoid a collision, during which manoeuvre the tow rope broke leaving the DFS 230 no option but to land. Piloted by Unteroffizier Pilz it not only had 8 troops on board but also Oberleutnant Witzig, the commander of group 'Granit'. Witzig climbed from the machine and ordered his men to remove all obstacles and create a makeshift runway. Witzig himself stopped a passing motorcar and went to Cologne-Ostheim in the hope

of obtaining a Ju 52. None was to be had there, and he requisitioned a machine from Gütersloh by telephone; now it was 0505 hours, and his group was due to land on Eben Emael 20 minutes later. The replacement JU 52 set course for Aachen, climbed and crossed the German frontier. The men of group 'Granit' assumed that their commander had already landed at Eben Emael. Meanwhile the Unteroffizier Brendenbeck, the pilot of the second DFS 230, believed he had made the target and so released his towing mechanism and landed. The men had an unpleasant surprise when they realized that they had not gone beyond Düren! This meant that of the eleven JU 52/DFS 230 pairs only nine remained. These operated their release mechanisms shortly after 0500 hours, and the DFS 230s landed at Eben Emael. The paratroopers jumped from the DFS 230 and proceeded with hollow charge projectiles and other weapons to put the defences of the fortress out of action. While this fight was in full progress a single transport glider came in to land; it carried Oberleutnant Witzig who had, after all, succeeded in catching up with his unit. He soon established radio contact with Hauptmann Koch, who had landed with group 'Beton' near Vroenhoven, and Oberstleutnant Mikosch and his Pioneer-Battalion 51, who proceeded more slowly. Witzig and his men succeeded in holding the fort. 'Beton' and 'Stahl' did the same, the latter mainly as a result of support by the Aldinger anti-aircraft battalion with its 8.8 cm Flak 36 AA guns, the Henschel Hs 123 fighter aircraft of II/LG2 and the Stukas of StG2.

The fight for Eben Emael ended on the following day at 1315 hours, when the Belgians in the fortress capitulated. German losses were within tolerable limits. The air landing operations in Holland, on the other hand, took an entirely different course. At 0500 hours 53 Ju 52s of I/KG zbV1 dropped paratroopers on both sides of the Moerdijk bridges, while at the same time 12 Ju 52s of I/KGr zbV172 deposited paratroopers at the Dordrecht bridges; subsequently 29 Ju 52s of the same group landed 4 km south of Dordrecht neat Wieldrecht. Punctually at 0500 hours, 53 Ju 52s of II/KG zbV1 dropped paratroopers at the airport Waalhaven/Rotterdam. A further 53 Ju 52s of III/KG zbv1 landed in and around Waalhaven; some were damaged by Dutch anti-aircraft fire and two crashed into the Maas. About 40 Ju 52s of KGr zbV9 landed along the Dordrecht-Moerdijk road. In the same area around Rotterdam a further 240 machines landed during the next day, some of which had initially been used for operations in the area of The Hague.

Here the airports of Valkenburg, Ockenburg and Ypenburg were the centres of operation, where air transport was mainly carried out by units working under KG zbV2. KG zbV1, under Oberst Morzik, had previously carried out some manoeuvres in conjunction with the 7th Flieger-Division and the 16th Infanterie-Regiment and, therefore, had some experience in carrying out such airborne operations. This was not the case with KG zbV2 under Oberst Conrad and the Luftlande-Infanterie-Division. The latter consisted of units that had only recently been amalgamated and was made up of flying school and Lufthansa crews.

In the area around The Hague the following events took place. At 0455 hours six JU 52s of 1/KGr zbV172 landed paratroopers. One was shot down by Dutch anti-aircraft artillery and crashed into the sea. One minute later five Ju 52s of KGr zbv12 dropped paratroopers south of Valkenburg airport. At 0520 hours 30 Ju 52s of KGr zbV11 came in to land at Valkenburg. Of these, one was shot down at 0520 hours near Veenendaal. Because the landing place was overcrowded, one machine landed at near-by Katwijk, a Dutch coastguard airfield from which it subsequently took off again. A second machine went to Ockenburg for similar reasons. Since the ground at Valkenburg was wet, the heavy Ju 52s were unable to take off and most of them were shot to pieces on the ground by the Dutch. Seven Ju 52s of KGr zbV12 also went to Ockenburg. Of the six Ju 52s of I/KG zbV1 coming from Werl one was shot down near Maaldrift, while the other five landed on the beach between Scheveningen and Wassenaare at 0935 hours. Eight machines landed at 0945 hours north of Wassenaare Slag and came under machine gun fire. Only one machine was subsequently able to take off. Ten minutes later five machines of the same unit landed on the beach near Scheveningen. In all, 20 Ju 52s returned with their cargo to Werl. Of six Ju 52s of KGr zbV9 five returned to their starting point, only one landing at Ockenburg as scheduled. A further 12 Ju 52s, of IV/KG zbV1, were also scheduled to land at Ockenburg. One was shot down west of Delft while on its approach, and although the remaining machines succeeded in dropping their paratroopers, they all crash-landed south of Ockenburg; they belonged to the second wave of KG zbV1 and had set out from Loddenheide. On the other hand, 17 Ju 52s of KGr zbV12 from Störmede succeeded in landing at Ockenburg and in depositing their infantrymen. Twenty-four Ju 52s of the second wave of KGr zbV9 from Bad Lippspringe were scheduled to land at Ockenburg at around 0605 hours. Of these, one came under fire and landed near Looschijnen, six were unable to land because the airfield was overcrowded, and three landed on the beach. Eleven Ju 52s of this group were scheduled to go to Ypenburg. Four landed around 0650 hours on the beach near Terheyde, two landed near the 'Solleveld' farmhouse at 0655 hours and succeeded in taking off again shortly afterwards. Two further machines came down at 0704 hours in the forests between Ockenrade and Ockenburg. One had the equipment for a complete field hospital on board. Three further machines landed at Ockenburg at 0702 hours. From there, five Ju 52s returned to Germany between 0800 and 0900 hours, taking with them 22 crew members of incapacitated machines. One Ju 52 was shot down by a Fokker

DXXI fighter plane near Stolwyk. Three machines, one of them belonging to KGr zbV11, destination Valkenburg, landed at Ockenburg, the other two made emergency landings on the beach. The third wave consisted of 12 Ju 52s of IV/KG zbV1 from Loddenheide, arriving around 0925 hours. Of these two landed north and south of Wassenaare Slag on the beach, together with 16 Ju 52s of I/KG zbV1 intended for Valkenburg. The remaining ten circled in the air and eventually flew on to Wallhaven. An initial 35 Ju 52s of IV/KG zbV1 appeared above Ypenburg airport. One was shot down near Rhenen, a second was hit by anti-aircraft fire and made an emergency landing near Delft, while a third was shot down near Rijswijk, the fourth near Escampolder and the fifth near Scheveningen, where it fell into the sea. The remaining machines returned to Germany, having deposited their paratroopers; one of them sustained 30 per cent damage during landing.

Thirty-six Ju 52s of KGr zbV12 also formed part of the first Ypenburg wave, and these arrived towards 0520 hours. Thirteen crash-landed or were destroyed by anti-aircraft fire — all these aircraft caught fire and only three men escaped, 206 lost their lives; 23 machines remained in the air. Seven landed at Valkenburg, three near Oude Leede, four alongside the Delft-Rotterdam road, three in the vicinity, two near Bleiswijk. Three were shot down near Plaspoelpolder, Delft and Abbswoude respectively. At 0605 hours the second wave arrived, consisting of 40 machines of KGr zbV9, among them one radio aircraft and one staff plane. Fourteen landed by the roadside south of Delft, 13 went to Ockenburg and five attempted to land, of which two subsequently made emergency landings near Molenbocht and just east of Ypenburg. Three landed northwest of Bleiswijk and eventually returned to Germany. The next five JU 52 fared little better: some were shot down, others destroyed after landing.

Two further machines of KGr zbV9 were shot down, one near Hoekpolder, the other in the area of Delft. Ten further machines landed at Ockenburg; one other was shot down near The Hague. Only 28 Ju 52s were available for the third wave intended for Ypenburg; these belonged to IV/KG zbV1. Of these 13 landed at Waalhaven, four at Oranjepolder, three at de Lange Bouwen, and two at Bankpolder. Three machines made emergency landings near Monster, south of Delft and near Rozenburg. One was shot down near Hillwoning. Two landed at Nordwestpolder, all the others either crashed or came under fire after landing. All these events took place between 1000 hours and 1105 hours. Finally, 38 Ju 52s of I/KGr zbV172, intended for Ypenburg, landed at Waalhaven after one had made an emergency landing at 1232 hours south of the road leading to Delft.

In the area around The Hague about 3325 infantrymen and some 500 air crew were on the ground spread over 14 different locations. The three airports of Ockenburg, Valkenburg and Ypenburg were recaptured by the Dutch during the course of the day. The losses of Ju 52 in this area (The Hague) alarmed Luftflotte 2 (Kesselring). The following telex was sent to Heeresgruppe B (General Oberst von Bock): '22 Division. Air landings at the airports Katwijk, Kijduin and Ypenburg apparently largely unsuccessful because of heavy ground and anti-aircraft action by the enemy. With few exceptions none returned of KGr zbV11 and 12 as well as I/KG 172. Radio contact has now been established with the staff of 22 Division'. The second sentence did not describe the reality. Only KGr zbV9, 11 and 12 recorded losses of 73 and 100 per cent while those of I/KGr zbV172 amounted to only 22 per cent. According to information issued by the quartermaster general of the Luftwaffe and Dutch sources KG zbV1 lost between 61 and 63 Ju 52s, KG zbV2 about 140 to 157 aircraft. With a total number of 430 aircraft deployed this is a loss rate of 51 per cent. This does not count damaged Ju 52s; about 100 machines were retrieved and later repaired. Although the Dutch had succeeded in recapturing the airports of the area around The Hague they did not destroy the aircraft landed at Valkenburg and Ockenburg. Although the Dutch commander-in-chief General Winkelmann signed a document as early as 15 May confirming the capitulation of all Dutch armed forces, which once again proved the value of such air landing operations, and although it had detracted attention from the action of German tanks in the Ardennes, it was nevertheless apparent at the end of the day that nearly half the German air transport capacity has been destroyed. General Walter Speidel commented: 'The loss of air transport capacity made itself felt for years afterwards'.

Despite heavy losses the transport pilots proved that they had become indispensible. The rapid advance of the tank units and the mo-

torized troops as well as the continuous relocation of airfields for all flying units would not have been possible without the JU 52. The remains of KG zbV1 and KGr zbv9 and 172 as well as the now available KGr zbV105 and 106 were on the wing day and night to move fuel, ammunition, bombs, and other equipment to the front. On return flights they always took wounded soldiers back to military hospitals. In addition, Ju 52s flying the Reichsdienstflagge, their tail units painted white with a red cross, were used as ambulance aircraft and for coast guard duties along the conquered coasts of Holland, Belgium and France. Meanwhile, Junkers and ATG tried to fill the gaps in the air transport fleet. The Ju 52s damaged in Holland were back in service after only a few weeks. The two Kamfgruppen zbV 11 and 12, however, which had been virtually annihilated were disbanded.

Cologne – Ostheim 10 May 1940: the first Ju 52/DFS 230 during take-off.

Climbing on their flight towards the Western Front, on course for Eben Eamel.

80

Left: **Using a long tow rope as late as 1940.**

Centre: **Having landed the transport gliders, the second wave brought the paratroopers into action.**

Bottom left: **Tirelessly, the Ju 52s flew one mission after another.**

Bottom right: **The Belgians and Dutch forever saw new groups of Ju 52s in the skies above them**

Paratroopers jumping in the Rotterdam area.

Ju 52 of KG zbV1 dropping paratroopers above Holland.

Airborne troops boarding a Ju 52.

82

At 0540 hours near Overschie (Holland), a crash-landed Ju 52 of KGr zbV9.

Ju 52 destroyed near Veenendal.

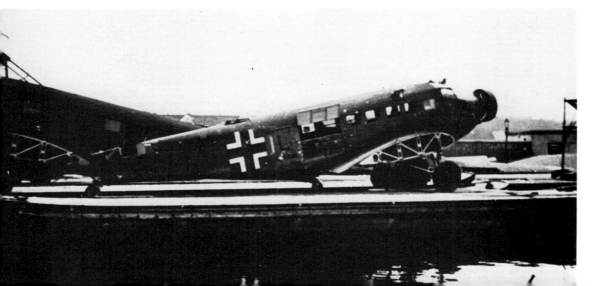

Recovered Ju 52 of KGr zbV9 on a pontoon near Laakkade.

83

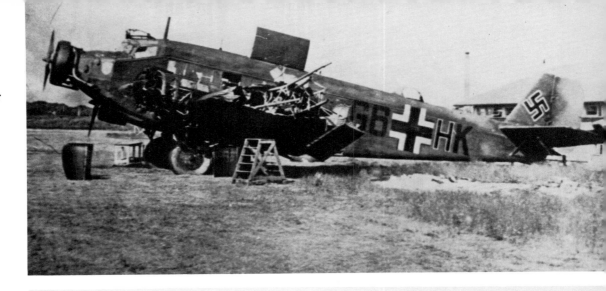

Damaged Ju 52 at Ockenburg airport near The Hague.

This Ju 52 crash-landed in a canal near Stolwyk.

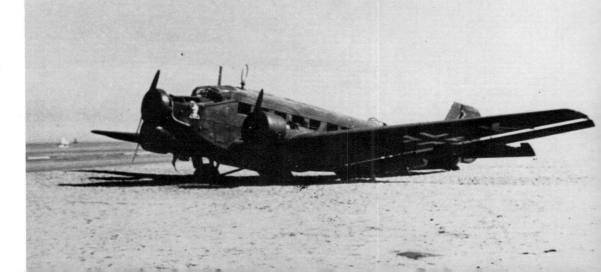

Emergency landing of a Ju 52 on Wassenaar beach (I/KG bV1).

84

The Dutch populace inspected with some satisfaction the smashed up Ju 52.

Ju 52 wrecks were scattered all along the Haagweg, the main road between Rijswijkoelft and Ypenburg. This picture shows machines of 11/KG zbV1.

Belly-landing near Ypenburg.

85

Dutch women
inspecting a damaged
Ju 52 near
Grubbevorst.

Recovery of a Ju 52 on
the road near
Ypenburg.

In France the activities
of the Ju 52 were
limited to supply
operations. On the
return flight wounded
soldiers were flown
back to Germany.

Unloading ammunition.

Again and again wounded soldiers who could only be treated at home were flown back.

Ju 52s were also used as messenger aircraft. In front of the machine a VW command car, type 62.

High-explosive bombs,
type SC250, for the
bomber groups also
had to be transported.

Continuous supplies of
ammunition were
required for the
advancing armoured
units.

The Western Campaign
is over. Ju 52s above
Rotterdam harbour.

From the Battle of Britain to the Balkan War 1940/41

The experience gained in the West and in Norway with Ju 52-3mg3e and g4e had resulted in further development work and the g5e version. This version was similar in part to the g4e and could be modified from land landing gear to floats, but was not suitable for dropping paratroops and air landing units, since it could not be fitted with conversion unit F. All other versions could be fitted with the following conversion units:

E = Loading device for crate transport
R = Seating for 16 passengers
H = Flying lecture room
St = Fittings to move ground personnel
S = Interior equipment for use as ambulance
F = Interior fittings for paratroopers

During the further course of the war new facilities were created for the additional installation of defence weapons.

In contrast to previous versions, the Ju 52-3mg5e had wings with a detachable smooth metal leading edge, which reached from the engine to the tip of the wing and which formed a hot air duct for de-icing the wings. The necessary warm air was supplied by the wing engines through heat exchangers. Some machines were also fitted with rubber de-icers, and all tail units were fitted with rubber de-icers. The propellers had been fitted with liquid de-icers. The intake air for the engines was pre-heated by an adjustable device. If necessary, towing devices for use with the Gotha Go 242 medium assault gliders could be fitted. When used as a floatplane the g5e could be fitted with 9500 or 11,000 litre floats, or with landing skis for winter conditions. It was armed with an MG131 and 4-5 MG15. The FuG 5a radio unit used initially was later replaced by the FuG 10 (TZG 10); furthermore, G5 direction finding units and more modern direction finding, radio and compass equipment were installed in all machines. During the course of 1941 three further important versions of the Ju 52-3m were built: the g6e, like the g5e with BMW 132T, but with wheels or landing skis only, and FuG 3aU radio equipment instead of FuG 5aU; the Ju 52-3mg7e transport aircraft for land and sea use, similar to the g5e but with a longer loading hatch, window modifications between vertical frames 5 and 6 and fitted with K4ü Siemens automatic pilot; and the Ju 52-3mg8e, similar to the g6e but with K4ü automatic pilot.

At the end of May 1940 the administrative department Lufttransportchef (Land) was renamed Lufttransportführer (LTF) by the quarter master general. On 2 July 1940 preparations started for the enterprise 'Operation Sea-Lion' with a directive to the supreme command of the army; Hitler had decided that 'under certain circumstances' a landing operation in Great Britain could be envisaged. On 9 July followed an order by Hitler under which the emphasis of German armaments efforts was to be on the sectors Luftwaffe and Navy. On 16 July followed 'Directive No. 16' to all three sections of the armed forces: preparation of a landing operation against Great Britain. Execution 'when necessary'! On 23 July the Wiesbaden Agreement between the Vichy government of France and the Reich was signed whereby French aircraft works were to build 200 aircraft for the German Luftwaffe. The firm of Amiot at Colombes began to produce Ju 52s. On 31 July Hitler started a controversial chain of actions which is difficult to explain. During a meeting with the Supreme Commander of the Kriegsmarine, Grossadmiral Raeder, he gave the date for the intended landing in Britain as 15 September. The definite date was to be fixed after one week's intensified air warfare against Britain. On the same day he announced to the Supreme Commander of the Army, Generalfeldmarschall von Brauchitsch, and his chief-of-staff, Generaloberst Halder, that he had decided to launch a five-month campaign against the Soviet Union in the spring of 1941. One wonders whether he was aware of the implications of carrying out the two operations. On 1 August 1940 'Directive No. 17', concerning intensified naval and air warfare against England, was issued, which was to lead to the Battle of Britain. On 27 August Hitler decided to carry out 'Operation Sea-Lion' in the form of a landing operation spread over 140 km of coast between Folkestone and Eastbourne. Two days later Raeder reported that the Kriegsmarine would not be ready to carry out 'Sea-Lion' before 20 September. At this time the chief of Luftwaffe training operations, General Kuhl, had moved all KG zbV units to France. KG zbV1 and 2 were already there. On 21 September the Royal Air Force destroyed 51 barges, nine steamships and one tug of the transport fleet that had been congregated at Le Havre and Antwerp in readiness for 'Sea-Lion'. On 26 September Raeder reported that it would be impossible to postpone 'Sea-Lion' until October. It was necessary to arrive at a decision. But Hitler had made other plans. 'Sea-Lion' was never to be carried out, since 15 Divisions were moved East on 6 September, while a further nine were were to follow by 5 October. All air transport units were moved back to the training schools, while KG zbV1 and 2 were made available for other tasks. As far as the Ju 52 units were concerned this marked the beginning of a deceptive lull.

In the meantime Mussolini, without informing Hitler, had started military operations which were to upset Hitler's plans for a long time to come. On 13 September the Italians, based in Lybia, attacked the British forces in Egypt, but their advance was halted as early as 18 September east of Sidi Barani. On 15 October the Italian War Council decided to attack Greece, an operation which started on 28 October, but by early as 2 and 3 November the Italians were repulsed. In Lybia, the Italians were under such great pressure that a German general, who had been sent there as an observer, urgently recommended on 3 November that a German Panzer unit should be sent to North Africa. As a result of Italian defeats in Greece, Hitler decided to carry out a diversionary attack on Greece through Hungary, Rumania and Bulgaria. In January 1941 KGr zbV40, 50 and 60 were formed from crews and aircraft of the flying schools. KGr zbV101, 104 and 105 which had already been in operation on the Western Front and in Norway, were re-assembled. This consolidation exercise was completed by February 1940. But as early as 20 December 1940 Hitler had taken the decision which was eventually to lead to his end and the fall of the Reich: he signed 'Directive No. 21', for 'Fall Barbarossa', the attack on the Soviet Union. Five days earlier an order had been given to attack Greece, 'Fall Marita'. The Greek troops had not only thrown back the Italians in November 1940 but had actually penetrated into Albania, at that time occupied by the Italians who urgently needed to bring in reinforcements. They did not, however, have the necessary naval or aircraft capacity. The Italian Supreme Command therefore asked the Germans for help. On 9 December the first 17 Ju 52s of III/KG zbV1 were moved from Graz and Wiener-Neustadt to Foggia. On the same day the Kriegstagebuch (war diary) of the Supreme Command of the Wehrmacht recorded that the position in the Balkans was impossible to assess. Yugoslavia was not prepared fully to join the three-power agreement between Germany, Italy and Japan, and Bulgaria also remained undecided. A full war in the Balkans became a distinct possibility. On 9 January 1941 Hitler decided to intervene in North Africa. This meant the establishment of a second front in the Mediterranean. The third front, in the East, was soon to follow.

90

After a thorough overhaul the old Ju 52-3mg3e's went to the flying schools.

Pilots in training.

Ju 52-3mg3e of Flugzeugführerschule (C), Lechfeld.

The curriculum of the
flying schools included
engine maintenance.

Ground crew of
KG zbV1 photographed
in front of a Ju 52 with
damaged landing gear.

The same machine
after crash-landing.

Ju 52-3m of the Halle-Nietleben radio operators' school.

A former Lufthansa Ju 52ge used for training.

Ju 52-3mg43 of the pilots' school B7.

93

A lot could happen during training: a damaged wing after a collision with another Ju 52.

Not all landings were as smooth as this one.

Bottom left: **During the Battle of Britain Ju 52s were used as search and rescue planes. Here a rescue squadron 'scrambles'.**

Bottom right: **Rescue planes were also used above the Baltic.**

The pilot of D-TABY keeping an eye on the neighbouring machine D-TABX.

Despite English fighter aircraft the rescue Ju 52s flew low to rescue fighter pilots.

Some rescue Ju 52s were armed to deter interference from enemy aircraft.

95

Ju 52s over the Balkans

From December 1940 onwards III/KG zbV1 using 53 Ju 52-3m's flew supply missions for the Italian troops in Albania. The parachute landing base at Foggia provided all necessary technical and other facilities so that no particular problems arose during these flights, which could only be carried out during daylight hours. Until the unit was moved to North Africa, where it flew supply missions for the German troops, the group flew, without losses, 1665 missions during which it transported Italian soldiers, and 2363 missions during which 2905 tonnes of materials were taken to Albania; on the return flights 10,970 men were flown back to Foggia.

On 6 February 1941 the operation 'Sonnenblume' began the transfer of German army units to North Africa. The first flight started on 8 February from Naples and was bound for Tripoli. Meanwhile, on 7 March, the first British troops landed at Volos and Piraeus, the harbour of Athens. Hitler's plans for the campaign against Greece and subsequently the USSR were upset by the coup d'etat in Belgrade on 27 March. On the same day he issued 'Directive No. 25': 'Yugoslavia is to be completely destroyed, both militarily and as a state'. Operation 'Barbarossa' was postponed. On 30 March the Africa Corps started its advance on Agedabia and thus the counter offensive against the British in Cyrenaica.

The chief of training for the Luftwaffe formed KGr zbV40, 50 and 60 from training units for the Balkans campaign against Yugoslavia and Greece. In addition KGr zbV101, 104 and 105 were formed at the beginning of February 1941. Initially their task consisted of ensuring the supply of Army and Luftwaffe units in the difficult Balkan mountains. They were under the command of the chief of the 11th Fliegerkorps. Early in April I and II/KG zbV1 and parts of KG zbV2 moved the 22nd Luftlande-Division from the area around Vienna to the Rumanian mineral oil area. KGr zbV104 was moved to Athens-Tatoi in April and placed under the 10th Fliegerkorps. On 17 April Yugoslavia had capitulated. The Greek armies were defeated, despite British assistance, to the extent that as early as 24 April the British forces instituted operation 'Demon' and started withdrawing their troops from Greece. In March and April 1941, II/KG zbV1 flew supplies to Tripoli and Benghazi, but subsequently left this task solely to III/KG zbV1 which had since the beginning of February been transporting supplies from Comiso in Sicily to North Africa.

Meanwhile the Balkans campaign was nearing its end. Even during this final phase, however, the Ju 52s of the KG zbV were to prove once again their worth. The commander of the 7th Flieger-Division, Generalleutnant Süssmann, was given the order to occupy the Isthmus of Corinth on both sides of the canal, using paratroops to defeat the enemy and secure the bridges across the canal for the more slowly advancing army units. For this purpose the following Ju 52 units were earmarked and gathered at Plodiv airport in Bulgaria: KG zbV2, I/LLG 1, I/KG zbV1, II/KG zbV1, KGr zbV60, KGr zbV 102,1 squadron using Ju 52-3m's with DFS 230 transport gliders and, as reserve, KGr zbV 101 and 172 as well as a small number of JU 52s under the command of Major Babekuhl. The first Ju 52s took off at 0500 hours on 26 April: after flying over the Pindus mountains the squadrons dropped down to 30 m above the Gulf of Corinth. The beginning of the canal was clearly visible, and the Ju 52s now climbed to the parachuting height of 120 m. Dive-bombers and bombers of the 12th Fliegerkorps had carried out the necessary softening-up bombardment, so that the paratroopers could be landed. Although the transport gliders did not succeed in securing the bridge the paratroop engineers, landed at the same time, were soon able to build an emergency bridge next to the one destroyed.

The Ju 52 groups flew back to Larissa. The Balkans War ended on 30 April 1941.

Large scale construction work of Ju52-3mg10e at the ex-Amiot works at Colombes near Paris.

Ju 52 of III/KG zbV1 transporting Italian troops to Albania.

Ju 52 of KG zbV2 in readiness at Plovdiv airport, Bulgaria.

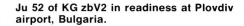

Agram airport, spring 1941, with Ju 52 *Nachtschwärmer* and Ju 87B-2 of 6/StG77.

Bucharest 1941: first on left, Horia Sima, leader of the Romanian fascists: (from fourth on left) Oberst Just; Marshal Antonescu; Oberst Gerstenberg; 7 General Werner Speidel; Ministerialrat Fabrizius. In the background is D-ATYZ, works number 5797.

Ju 52 on its way to Corinth.

98

Parachuting over Corinth.

Paratroopers jumping at short intervals from their Ju 52.

Paratroopers and their weapon containers dropping from a height of 120 m.

The transport gliders did not succeed in preventing the bridge from being blown up.

Operation 'Mercury'
– the last big airborne operation

A large part of the British force evacuated from Greece during Operation 'Demon' had been taken to Crete, and the Germans greatly underestimated the defensive forces of that island, which was under the command of General Freyberg. The estimated figure was between 7000 and 20,000, while in actual fact 42,640 soldiers were in Crete, ready for action. What Freyberg needed more than anything were aircraft and tanks and despite intensive German air attacks on the British supply fleet between 29 April and 20 May 1941 the British succeeded in getting around 15,000 tonnes of supplies to Crete. As early as 20 April General Student, the commanding General of the 11th Fliegerkorps had outlined the problem concerning Crete to Göring during a meeting. Göring, who agreed with Student's plan of first taking Crete, then Cyprus, in order to establish a spring-board to the Suez Canal, submitted this strategy to Hitler on the following day; he in turn agreed immediately. His view: 'Crete must be taken. There is another important reason: it is at any time possible to attack, from the British bases on Crete, the oil fields in Romania on which we depend. Please take all necessary steps'.

Göring instructed the chief of Luftflotte, Generaloberst Löhr, to assume command of the operation 'Merkur' (Mercury). Its actual execution became the task of General Student and his 11th Fliegerkorps. Air support was to be provided by the 13th Fliegerkorps under General von Richthofen. Ten transport units, all equipped with Ju 52-3m's, were made available for transport purposes and for towing transport gliders. These were I and II/KG zbV1, I/LLG1 and KGr zbV 101, 102, 105, 106, I/KGr zbV 172 as well as KGr zbV 40 and 60. Two different figures were given for the total number of Ju 52s used. One

source speaks of 493, the other of 502. Added to these were 85 transport gliders, mainly DFS 230s. Student's main problem during the preparations of operation 'Merkur' was the distribution of the air transport fleet, which had to carry out three different functions: the dropping of paratroops, the towing and releasing of transport gliders, and the transport of army units. The already mentioned transport units were distributed over the airfields or Corinth, Megara, Tanagra, Topolis, Dadion, Phaleron and Eleusos. Between 1 and 10 May 1941 the paratroop assault regiment and the remainder of the 7th Flieger-Division, the main part of which had been in Greece since the operation near Corinth, were brought to the scene of action. Instead of the initially intended 22nd Infanterie-Division Student was allocated the 5th and parts of the 6th Gebirgedivision (Mountain division). Parts of the 8th Fliegerkorps caused considerable havoc among the supply units for Crete before the operation started and sank half the supply ships used for this purpose. The fighter units Jagdgeschwader 77 and Zerstörergeschwader 26 destroyed all enemy aircraft in Crete. On 20 May 1941 starting at 0715 hours the landing operation started in three groups. Group 'West' landed at Maleme under Generalmajor Meindl, the central group landed at Chania and Suda under Generalleutnant Süssmann, who was killed during the approach to the landing site, while group 'East' landed at Erakleion under Generalmajor Ringel. Meindl was badly wounded. The 51-year-old Generalmajor Ramcke subsequently assumed the command over group 'West'.

During the first few days of this operation the situation was, at times, extremely dangerous. Considerable losses of transport aircraft occurred, many Ju 52s being destroyed by artillery during the landing operations at Maleme when the reinforced 5th Gebirgedivision (Mountain Division) was flown in by KG zbV1.

During this first week the main emphasis of air transport was on flying in combat troops with supply transports taking second place. With the expansion of active combat the demand for supplies of all types increased, since the initial provisions of food, ammunition, etc were soon used up. On 27 May the position in Crete had established itself in favour of the German units. On 27 May 1941, at 1500 hours, Crete's capital, Khania, was in German hands. The British side ceased its efforts to bring reinforcements to Crete. On the evening of 27 May 1941 General Freyberg received permission to pull out of Crete. Between 27 and 31 May a total of 17,000 Greek and British soldiers were evacuated from Crete, mainly during the night. Losses on both sides were high: the British and Greeks lost around 17,000 men, the Germans, 6,580. The worst losses, from a tactical point of view, were those of aeroplanes and transport units: 151 wrecked Ju 52-3m's were lying on Cretan airstrips! The Luftwaffe used the term 'aeroplane graveyard Crete'. Many crews had succeeded in baling out before their machines were destroyed. Since it was not possible to ensure a safe sea-link to Crete, all supplies had to be brought in by air until the end of June. Until 30 June the Ju 52s of KGr zbV carried out daily between 200 and 240 supply missions. Once sea transport started, the transport units were withdrawn. One part now became engaged in supplying German troops in North Africa.

As a side line to 'Merkur' another operation was initiated along the lines of operations intended by Student for the Near East but which, because of a lack of interest on the part of the German government, came to nothing. In Iraq the anti-British government of Ghailani had come to power, had sent troops to surround the British airbase at Habaniya and now asked for German help to expel the British. This was a unique opportunity to gain a foothold in the Near East. But Hitler's interests were concentrated on a different region: the Soviet Union. Only 10 Ju 52s and three four-engine Ju 90s were sent to Iraq, as well as six He 111s of KG4 'General Wever' for the attack on Habaniya. They carried out six bomb attacks by 29 May as well as seven reconnaissance flights. The operation was broken off on 31 May 1941.

Preparation of operation 'Merkur': first on left, Generalmajor Korten, chief-of-staff Luftflotte 4; (from fifth on left) General Student; Generaloberst Löhr; Generalmajor Schlemm.

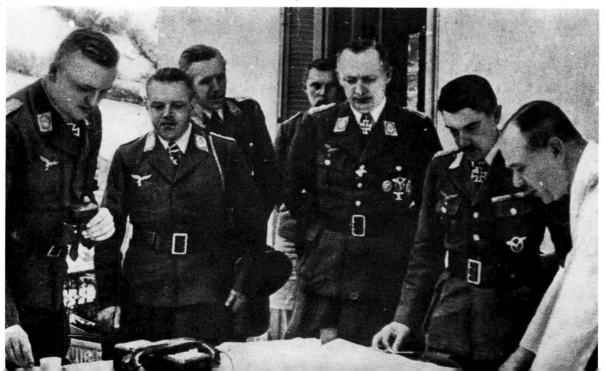

Top: **Ju 52 with DFS 230 in tow taking off from Athens – Eleusis on 20 May 1941.**

Middle: **Pairs of Ju 52 and DFS 230 taking off from Eleusis at short intervals.**

Right: **Ju 52 of 9/KGr zbV9 and Ju 87R-2 of II StG2 on their way to Crete.**

Ju 52 of 8/KG zbV1 above Greece.

Another Ju 52 belonging to same unit flying low above the Mediterranean.

Crete, 20 May 1941: two Ju 52s after landing; the shadow of a third shows that it too is about to touch down.

103

Ground personnel of 8/KG zbV1 testing the towing device.

Maleme, Crete, 26 May 1941: wrecked Ju 52s.

Maleme turned into a Ju 52 graveyard.

104

Ju 52s and other German
aeroplanes shot down by the
British.

This Ju 52 had been damaged
so badly over Crete that it
broke up when landing at
Eleusis.

Ju 52 of 8/KG zbV1 in
Sardinia.

Sleep comes easily after incessant missions.

Hospital aircraft were kept busy during the actions in Crete.

After Crete: Victory parade of the 1st Paratroop Regiment at Stendal; in front, Oberst Brauer, regiment commander.

106

Ju 52s fly supplies for Rommel

At the beginning of June 1941 all Ju 52 units with the exception of I/LLG1 had been removed from the Cretan operation. KGr zbV40 and 60 were disbanded. Preparations by the Wehrmacht for their attack on the USSR had been in full swing since 10 June. Other Ju 52s were used in an altogether different theatre of war; these were the Ju 52s supplied to South African Airways before the war and now used for flying supplies to the South African troops who were fighting against the Italians. Ju 86s refitted for use as bombers were also employed there.

In North Africa III/KG zbV1 flew on supply missions for the Afrikakorps, operating initially from Comiso in Sicily. After the 15th Panzer Division had landed in Tripoli on 31 March and Rommel's offensive had started with the conquest of Agedabia on 2 April, this group became everybody's 'Man Friday'. It flew supplies, carried out troop movements, and took, on its return flights, wounded soldiers to military hospitals. As a result it had to change constantly its bases in Sicily, Greece, and Africa. In March and April group II of KG zbV1 took part in these missions. The aircraft flew, without the protection of fighter planes, always operating at least 50 m above the sea, after it had been discovered that Ju 52s could easily be detected by the patrolling British Beaufighters as a result of a black 'wake' appearing on the surface of the water as a result of air disturbance. Nevertheless, no great losses occurred, although anti-aircraft guns on Italian ships were a nuisance; the Italian gunners were so nervous that they shot at any aircraft approaching their ship. All reports of the Ju 52 units went to the 10th Fliegerkorps under whose command they came. Flying operations were often made difficult by engine trouble. Additional oil coolers as well as sand and dust filters were no longer sufficient. Some of the crews started to suffer from gastro-enteritis, a result of the unfamiliar climate. At the same time a Luftverbindungs (LV)-Gruppe, a liaison unit of Ju 52 and other aircraft, was established, which was available to all army units for courier and service flights. When the British forces attempted to bypass the positions of the German 5th Light Infantry and 15th Panzer Divisions at the Lybian/Egyptian border, increased demand for supplies arose for the Afrikakorps. The British attempt failed on 17 June; as a result General Wavell was replaced by General Auchinleck as British commander-in-chief Middle East.

It now became apparent that the losses incurred by the air transport units in the West in 1940 and Crete in 1941 had been too heavy to be made up by increased production. As a result a new practice came into being which consisted of gathering Ju 52s, whenever the need arose, from wherever aircraft and crews were available and forming them into Kampfgruppen zbV on an *ad hoc* basis. Because of the urgency that always prevailed, these assembly operations were carried out overnight, and crew secondments were often poorly recorded. This meant that nobody knew exactly where aircraft and crews were deployed so that in a case of loss nobody knew who should be informed until some training school or unit reported a missing aircraft and crew. In view of the constantly rising need for transport some of the officers appointed had been rejected by other units as 'unsuitable' material. Some of those who were in charge of transport units did not even possess a pilot's licence! The number of old hands fell at an alarming rate, and not until the establishment of the 14th Fliegerkorps in 1943 were the transport flying units once again properly organized. Despite preparations for operation 'Barbarossa' improvisations continued on a large scale. Around this time, in spring 1941, the first prototype of a modernized Ju 52, the Ju 252 V1, was built at Dessau. As early as autumn 1938 it had been realized that with the appearance of the Heinkel He 111, Ju 86 and in particular the American Douglas DC 2, from which later the famous DC 3 was developed, the era of corrugated metal construction had come to an end, despite its undisputed advantages. In December 1938 the design office had completed the first plans of a replacement for the Ju 52, which was given the designation EF 72. These plans, which were for a transport plane for six first class passengers and 15 second class passengers, were rejected by Lufthansa and by the Reichsluftfahrtministerium's technical office. In July 1939 work on revising these plans started at Dessau, after Lufthansa had specified its requests and co-ordinated them with RLM. In addition, the technical department of RLM now fixed the type designation: Ju 252. Because of the outbreak of the war development work came to a halt. Only after the campaign in the West,

when the German leadership was convinced of total victory by Germany and an early peace, did RLM order the Ju 252 to be developed in an enlarged version for 32 passengers. The final plans were subsequently approved by Lufthansa and RLM. Work consequently started at Dessau on the construction of the first three prototype aircraft, Ju 252 V1, V2 and V3, during the spring of 1941. The Junkers branch at Bernburg, originally the hangars of Bernburg air base, was used for making components, although these works were actually intended for the final assembly of Ju 88s. The fact that Ju 252 was intended for military purposes became apparent by the inclusion of a so-called transport ramp at the rear end of the fuselage floor, such as had been incorporated in the Ju 90 V7 and V8. This arrangement made it possible to drive heavy weapons, cars and small armoured vehicles straight into the fuselage. Ju 252 V1 was completed by late autumn 1941.

Ju 52 of III/KG zbV1 at Comiso, Sicily; in the foreground on the right an Italian Savoia SM 79.

Ju 52g7e VK + AZ, with open loading hatches.

Ju 52 of Oberst Fritz Morzik, who died in 1985.

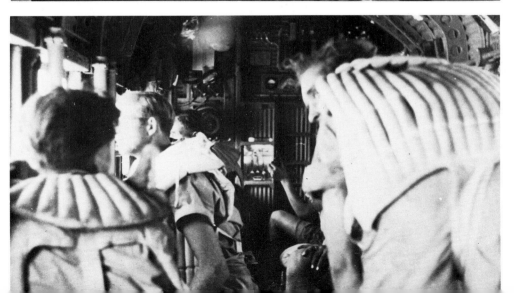

On the flight to North Africa the soldiers had to wear life jackets.

109

Over the African coast.

Landing at Benghazi.

Unloading a Daimler-Benz DB 605 for Bf 109 of JG27. From the recumbent forms in the foreground and flat tyre on the truck it might be assumed that the operation was brought to a halt by enemy intervention.

110

Ju 52-3mg7e of IV/KG zbV1
(there was a dust particle in
the camera!)

Squadron insignia of
8/KG zbV1.

Personal Insignia of Feldwebel Goers, 8/KG zbV1.

111

Ju 52 of KG zbV9 at
Elmas, Sardinia.

Ju 52 of 8/KG zbV1
also in Sardinia.

The landing gear broke
while landing in Sardi-
nia.

Ju 52 of KG zbV1 at Comiso, Sicily.

Ju 52 BG+ZJ at Forli (Italy).

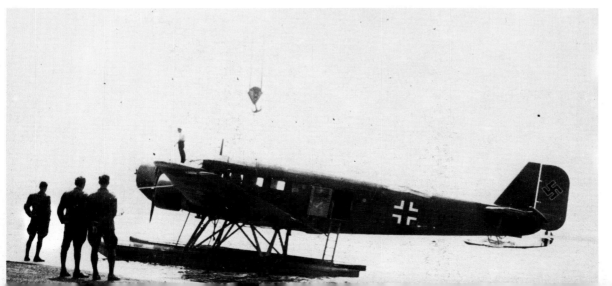

Ju 52-3mg7e of the maritime air transport squadron at Orbetello.

113

Ju 52-3mg7e of the maritime air transport squadron above the Aegean sea.

This Ju 52 of II/KG zbV1 on a special mission during the battle for Tobruk.

The Allies also used Ju 52s as transport planes. These were machines supplied to South Africa before the war and later used by the South African Air Force.

A model of EF 72, the
first version of Ju 252,
in a wind tunnel.

Ju 252 V1 leaving the
assembly hall at
Dessau for its first
flight.

Ju 252 V1 during a test
flight.

Ju 52s in the East and the Mediterranean – up to the end of 1941

The Air Fleets participating in operation 'Barbarossa' were allocated the following transport units equipped with Ju 52:

Luftflotte 5, Scandinavia	KGr zbV108
Luftflotte 1, Northern Section	KGr zbV106
Luftflotte 2, Centre	KGr zbV102
	(under Flying Corps II)
Luftflotte 4, South East	KGr zbV50 and 54

In other words, 200 transport planes were available for a front which was around 5000 km long. The rapid advance of the Panzer units and their necessary supplies of fuel, ammunition and provisions presented the flying units with increasingly difficult problems, especially as early losses occurred as a result of Soviet anti-aircraft fire and fighter plane attack. As early as 5 July, in other words two weeks after the start of the German offensive on 22 June 1941, the Supreme Command of the Wehrmacht reported the total loss of 171 reconnaissance, liaison and transport aircraft. A further 87 aircraft of this type were badly damaged.

How far the undisputed German successes were overrated by the German leadership can be seen by the fact that the Chief of the General Staff of the Army, Generaloberst Halder, regarded the campaign in the East as having been decided by 9 July 1941. He did not know that on 2 August the USA had started supplying the Soviet Union with war *matériel*. On 8 August the battle of encirclement near Uman ended in the annihilation of the 6th, 12th, and parts of the 18th, Soviet armies. This victory was the cause for Hitler to visit, together with his ally Mussolini, the southern army units at Berdichev, in order to demonstrate his success to Mussolini. Compared with the two Focke-Wulf Fw 200s, in which they travelled, the Ju 52 used by the generals and marshalls also present at this inspection looked somewhat modest. In the Mediterranean the British forces with their superior naval forces successfully intercepted missions bringing supplies to Rommel's troops in North Africa.

In the Far East the Japanese navy had started a war game under the command of the Commander-in-Chief of the United Fleets, Admiral Yamamoto. Plans for a war in the Pacific took shape. Around the same time an order was given to draw a demarcation line between the functions of air transport units and those of the 11th Fliegerkorps. This was only partly implemented for not until the autumn were all KGr zbV removed from the 11th Fliegerkorps. It had become apparent that the transport capacity of the five KG zbV made available on 22 June 1941 was not sufficient. Each flying corps now had a group and each army corps a squadron of transport aircraft.

On 1 October 1941 the former director of Deutsche Lufthansa, Karl August von Gablenz, by then Oberst and Lufttransportführer, became the head of the planning department within RLM, but on 21 August 1941 he was killed when his Siebel Fh 104 crashed during a flight from Berlin to Prien (Chiemsee). His successor was Oberst Fritz Morzik. Morzik had for a long time been flying instructor at DVS and had also made a name for himself as a sporting pilot, by winning European flying competitions in 1929 and 1930.

With the exception of KG zbV1 all Ju 52 units were now employed on the Eastern Front. On 18 November 1941 a British counter offensive started in North Africa, which forced bombers to abandon the attack on the encircled Tobruk. The result was an increased demand for air transport capacity both in the East and in the Mediterranean area and, once again, the Luftwaffe

116

schools suffered depletion. The Luftwaffe Chief of Training had to form the new KGr zbV300, 400 and 500 by 10 December 1941 from the special flying schools. Some of the airborne forces units also had to give up machines and crews. When cold weather in Russia meant that hardly any supplies could be moved on the ground, KGr zbV600, 700, 800, 900 and 999 were formed from personnel from the same sources. Oberst Morzik himself took over the task of carrying out air supplies on the Eastern Front with a special staff. KGr zbV400 and 500 were formed with half the normal strength and moved to Foggia, Brindisi and Trapani.

By the end of 1941 the following Ju 52 units were in the Mediterranean area:

III/KG zbV1
KGr zbV400
KGr zbV500
Transport squadron of the Afrikakorps
Transport squadron of the 10th Fliegerkorps

KGr zbV400 and 500 brought new personnel from both army and air force from Naples and Palermo to Tripoli, the other transport squadrons were used only for supplying the troops. On their return flights the wounded, and Italian refugee families, were taken to Italy. One squadron of III/KG zbV1 supplied the islands of Crete and Rhodes from Athens-Tatoi. Since the crews of the newly formed transport units were young and inexperienced – and they had been sent to the front without being adequately trained – losses were heavy. KGr zbV400, for example, lost eleven machines with their crews within a short period of time. Since it was not possible to get sufficient supplies to the Afrikakorps by sea, Rommel's units were forced to retreat further and further. To compound the problem KGr zbV500 was sent to the Eastern Front despite the difficult transport situation. During the retreat in North Africa around 9,000 German and Italian soldiers were bottled-up between Sollum and the Halfaya Pass during November/December 1941. They had to be supplied by air, and this was only possible at night. Major Friedl Fath, Staffelkapitän of III/KG zbV1, who had previously been chief pilot with Dornier, was in charge of this special unit. The operational centre for the two squadrons of KG zbV1 was Tympakion, Crete. Only experienced pilots could be used for these 'blind' flights. During the course of this operation nine Ju 52s were lost, two further crashed soon after taking off from Tympakion. In spite of deployment of the transport planes it was not possible to prevent the capitulation of the encircled units. On 7 December Generalfeldmarschall Rommel gave up the fight for Tobruk and retreated to the Gazala line. On the same day the Japanese attacked Pearl Harbour.

Oberst von Gablenz (Director of Lufthansa).

General Fritz Morzik.

General Major der Flieger Kuhl , the Luftwaffe chief of training. KG zbV were formed from aircraft operating under his command.

Ju 52 belonging to the staff of KG zbV9.

Ju 52s of KG zbV1 above the Mediterranean.

Ju 52 4U + BR of KGr zbV172 in Italy.

118

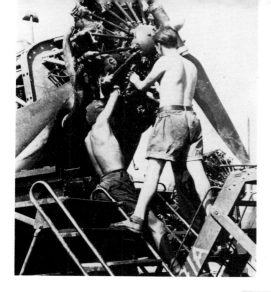

Engine repairs in Sicily, at temperatures of 95 degrees Farenheit in the shade.

Crash-landing of a Ju 52-3m 1Z + F of KG zbV1, in Sicily.

Ju 52-3m-g7e coming into land at Elmas.

119

USSR 1941. In view of their rapid advance the Luftwaffe units had to constantly move their operational bases. This would have been impossible without Ju 52s. Here is the Ju 52 6M+QL of Reconnaissance Squadron 3.(F)11.

The Witebsk airfield, 1941.

Ju 52 of IV/KG zbV1 at Witebsk, 1941.

Ju 52 of the courier squadrons were available to higher ranks.

Ju 52-3mg7e, works number 6753, loading fuel.

Ju 52-3m's waiting for cargo for the return flight. Some soldiers wait also, hoping to get a lift; in the foreground a typical Russian cart.

Transporting mail was also one of the jobs of the Ju 52.

Horses and carts were indispensable means of transport between air landing strips and the troops. This Ju 52 came from a school and was moved to a KG zbV.

Ju 52-3m, works number 5379, belonging to 2/KGr zbV800.

122

Landing gear repairs under difficult circumstances.

Crash-landings were not unusual in Russia.

The early onset of winter in 1941 brought unexpected problems.

Starting engines during the Russian winter became a problem.

This Ju 52 of flying school B8, Wiener-Neustadt, had seen active service during the Balkan war.

The Ju 52MS 'Mausi'

A report on the origins of this version of the Ju 52 was given in a letter dated 19 April 1985 by Th. Benecke, a high-ranking civil servant who, after 1945, held a high position in the Federal German Ministry of Defence:

'In September 1939 I stayed with the navy's test unit at Kiel when news was received of an English magnetic mine found in the Kattegat. An examination of the inductive magnetic system led to the conclusion that this ignition system responded to an artificial magnetic field. I discussed the matter with the physicist Professor Gerlach in Munish and made the suggestion that a Ju 52 should be fitted with a horizontally arranged coil ring with a diameter of about 14 m. I was able to calculate the magnetic field created by a current passed through the annular cable since I had done work with Helmholtz coils at the Institute for Experimental Physics at Kiel University. The chief of the technical department within RLM gave me priority, and within five weeks a Ju 52 was fitted with a 14 m diameter ring, containing 44 windings of an aluminium cable. A Leonard power unit from a searchlight battery, fitted into the Ju 52, provided the necessary current, and we flew to Vlissingen, where the harbour approaches were full of mines, dropped by the British from aeroplanes. Success was instant! We flew at a height of 10 to 20 m above the surface of the water, and the mines exploded about 200 to 300 m behind the aircraft, since the mines had been fitted with a seven second delay switch. I was presented with a special award by the Generalluftzeugmeister, Generaloberst Udet, handed to me by him personally, as a reward for designing the Ju 52MS, code name 'Mausi' and its first successful mission'.

In his memoirs Ernst Zindel also reports on this 'interesting and unusual special version of the Ju 52'.

'This was a Ju 52-3mg4e or g6e fitted, for clearing mines, with a large electro-magnetic loop, known as 'Mausischleife'. A large magnetic ring was suspended below wings and fuselage; this consisted of 64 [sic] turns of aluminium wire of a diameter of about 10 mm and an average diameter of each turn of about 14.30 m, which corresponded to an overall length of around 3000 m of aluminium wire. The wire coils were held in place by plywood struts suitably bored and were enclosed in aerodynamic sheet metal fairings of about 35 cm depth and 10 cm thickness; the outer diameter of this magnetic ring was about 14.60 m. The aerodynamic effects of the ring, which was after all, of considerable size, being nearly as long as the entire Ju 52 fuselage, whose diameter was half the wing span and whose surface area of 18 sq m amounted to nearly one sixth of the wing surface of the Ju 52, were tested in a wind tunnel before being fitted. The electric energy was provided by a 150 Kw generator housed in the fuselage and driven by a petrol or diesel engine. With care it was possible to keep within tolerable limits the aerodynamic effects caused by the enormous ring. However, it cannot have been a pleasant feeling for the aircraft crews to fly, with their Ju 52 complete with 'Mausischleife', at a height of 50 m or less over magnetic minefields, with mines exploding about 5 m behind them. The first mine disposal unit came into being as early as 1940 under the name 'Sonderkommando Mausi'; from it emerged later the first mine location group. Modification work for the first Ju 52 g4e took place at a works air base near the Dresden-Neustadt air station'.

After the campaign in the West, Minensuch-gruppe No. 1 (Mine Detection Unit) was moved to Holland. The individual squadrons were distributed at varying locations as far as the West Friesian Islands. This was due to the fact that

German convoys heading for the Atlantic coast travelled between the coast and the islands, and this is where British submarines patrolled and aircraft dropped their mines at night. The activities of the British mine layers extended far beyond the Friesian coast. It became necessary to base mine sweepers at Grossenbrode, Warnemünde, and Cammin, in order to cope with mines laid in the bays of Kiel and Lübeck and the Pomeranian coast from Stettin to Penemünde. The main area in which the constantly growing number of mine detection units became active was the French Atlantic coast. Mine detection commands were at Vannes near Lorient, St. Nazaire, and La Rochelle. From the base at Cognac, the area from the river mouth of the Gironde to Bordeaux was covered. In order to secure ore transports from Spain, a mine detection command was sent to Biarritz. Re-

peated losses occurred through the action of British 'Beaufighters', since the Ju 52 MS's only defence weapon consisted of an MG15 fitted in the back of the fuselage, and since they had to fly without the protection of fighter planes. The majority of units consisted of four aircraft and their crews, led by a senior NCO. He took part in all missions and also had to deal with the resulting paperwork. Comradeship and co-operation among the crews were excellent. How many mine detection commandos using these JU 52MS existed in all, can no longer be ascertained.

The start of operation 'Barbarossa' necessitated the constant formation of new 'Mausi' units. They were in operation everywhere from the Atlantic to the Black Sea, and they were to remain active after the ceasefire in 1945.

Ju 52-3mg7e KI + LQ of a mine detection unit in Lybia.

Even an old Lufthansa JU 52 had been promoted to mine detector.

Front mounting of the magnetic ring on the fuselage of the Ju 52.

In the air the 'Mausi' presented a strange spectacle.

127

Ju 51-3mg6e of Mine Location Group 1 above
the Mediterranean.

The stripes on the tail unit indicate the number
of missions flown by this crew.

A 'Mausi' starts its hunt

This photograph taken from a Ju 52 clearly shows how closely the mines detonated behind the 'Mausi' (Baltic sea).

This photograph shows how low a Ju 52 had to fly to detonate the mines.

129

Airlift Demyansk, spring 1942

On 3 January 1942 part of the 216 Infanterie-Division, about 4000 men, were encircled near Sukhinichi by the 10th Soviet Army. For the first time an entire army unit had to be supplied from the air until its relief on 24 January, for which about 40 Ju 52s were sufficient. On 9 January 1942 two, and after 15 January three, Soviet armies, advanced from the Ostanshkov region over the Waldai mountains, broke through between the German army groups 'North' and 'Centre' and encircled Kholm on 22 January. Meanwhile a far greater catastrophe loomed: on 18 January 1942 the 34th and 11th Soviet Armies closed the ring around the 2nd German Army Corps under General von Brockdorff-Ahlefeld and large sections of the 10th Army Corps. As a result about 95,000 men were surrounded in the Demyansk region. General von Brockdorff-Ahlefeld had immediately realized what problems lay ahead and requested on 24 January from Supreme Army Command (AOK) 16: 'Please send by air, troops capable of moving under winter conditions and at least 200 tonnes of supplies daily. For the last fortnight troops have received only two-thirds and the horses one-third of allocated rations.' This outlined the task ahead for the transport planes. On 18 February Oberst Morzik was given the order to move his operational staff to Luftflotte 1. The Lufttransportführer (LTF) thus came under the command of the head of Luftflotte 1, Generaloberst Keller (during the First World War chief of Bombengeschwader 1 and subsequenly of Deutsche Verkehrsfliegerschule (DVS) in Braunschweig). It was decided that the daily minimum requirement of supplies for the Demyansk pocket was 300 tonnes. On 19 February IV/KG zbV1 and KGr zbV600, 700, 800 and 900 joined KGr zbV172 and 9, already under the command of Luftflotte 1. The following units of Luftflotte IV were moved to Luftflotte 1 at the end of February: II/KG zbV1 and KGr zbV500, 'Posen' and 'Oels', as well as sections of KGr zbV105. At the beginning of March the following units were newly formed from training schools: KGr zbV4, 5, 6, 7 and 8. These, too, were used to fly supplies to Demyansk.

All these units, with the exception of KGr zbV5, who were flying He 111, were equipped with Ju 52. The quality of the crews varied greatly. Next to old and experienced transport pilots, young and inexperienced crews were used, which had been sent off without finishing their training. Nevertheless, these young units turned out to be useful, since they rapidly adapted themselves to actual conditions. The bases were Pleskau West, Pleskau South, Korovyu-Selov, Riga, Riga North, Dunaburg, and Tuleblya. Each of these places was allocated a JU 52 workshop section, but supplies of engines and spare parts were slow to arrive, never meeting demand, and many of the badly damaged aircraft were used for spares. Most of the operations had to be carried out without the protection of fighter planes; as a result, they were usually flown in staggered formation, so that individual machines could cover each other. Repeated losses occurred after attacks by low-flying Soviet Stormovik (Ilyushin Il-2). Since during the first week Oberst Morzig had only 75 serviceable JU 52s, AOK 16 released KG4 for operations at Demyansk. The bombers of KG4 (He 111H-6) were not used for bombing missions but for dropping supply containers. The He 111 also flew to Kholm, where landing facilities existed only infrequently and thus enabled Generalmajor Scherer, the commander at Kholm, and his men to hold out until relief arrived. On 20 February 1942 the first 40 Ju 52s landed at Demyansk airport. While they were being unloaded, the gunners of the JU 52s remained at their posts, ready to fire, since there was always a risk of attack by low-flying Soviet aircraft. Apart from a small number of 2 cm Flak 38 and Flak-MGs no protection was available for the transport planes. A provisional landing place inside the enclosed pocket, 12 km north of Demyansk, near Pyesky, could only be used by highly experienced pilots. Moreover, because of the size the Ju 52s were unable to take more than 1500 kg of supplies to that location; it is believed, though, that wounded soldiers were taken back on the return flights. The Demyansk airlift lasted for more than three months, until, on 28 April, ground units succeeded in establishing contact with the encircled troops.

Every available machine was used for the relief of the troops at Demyansk. Lufthansa had to give up nearly all available aircraft, and these included the large Ju 90 and Fw 200. Hitler even sent a Fw 200, which had been intended for his personal use, to Demyansk, as well as his pilot Hansl Baur. After the breakthrough KGr zbV8 and 999 were disbanded. They returned to their training schools. IV/KG zbV1, which had operated as KGr zbV 'Posen' during the Demyansk airlift, and KGr zbV500, which had been given the code name 'Oels', became once again known by their former designations.

Demyansk had shown the extent to which army units could be supplied by the massed use of air transport units, but it had also shown that those in charge of supplies were not sufficiently familiar with the potential of air transport. The success of Demyansk led to an overrating of such possibilities by Göring and, as a result of his reports, by Hitler and thus contributed to the catastrophe of Stalingrad.

At around this time, in spring 1942, a new version of the Ju 52, the g9e, was built at Dessau. It was largely identical with the g8e, but could only be used as a land aircraft. All machines were fitted with BMW 132Z engines and were equipped with two MG131s, had standard loading hatches on the right-hand side of the fuselage, towing devices for transport gliders, landing gear strengthened for a take-off weight of 11,500 kg, and the following radio equipment: FuG 10 with TZG 10, 'Peil G' direction finder, FuB1 2H, FuG 101 and FuG 25. Work started immediately on the large-scale production of this model.

The performance of the transport aircraft used for supplying Demyansk was unsurpassed: between 20 February and 21 April 1942 64,844 tonnes of supplies and 30,500 soldiers were flown to Demyansk during 33,086 misions, and 35,400 wounded were taken back on the return flights. 387 members of the flying crews, mainly from Ju 52s, lost their lives. This meant the loss of about 100 crews!

The chief of Luftflotte 1, Generaloberst Keller.

KG zbV500 ready for action at Tuleblya.

Further Ju 52s had been requisitioned from the schools to supply Demyansk. In the foreground two Ju 52s of Instrument Flying School 2, Neuburg/Danube, in the background a Ju 52 of KGr zbV500; Pleskau South, 22 February 1942.

This Ju 52 was requisitioned from the Aircraft Radio Operators School Halle-Nietleben.

In the foreground, a Ju 52 of Instrument Flying School B36, Gardelegen, in the background a Ju 52 of KGr zbV500, destroyed by low-flying Soviet aircraft.

Ju 52 of KGr zbV500 flying low on its way to Demyansk.

An aircraft gunner behind his MG15 carefully scanning the sky for Russian fighter planes.

Pleskau, July 1942. In the centre Major Beckmann, commander of KGr zbV500; third from right the commander of the Spanish Blue Division, General Munoz Grande.

Major Beckmann, during a flight to Demyansk. He was awarded the Ritterkreuz for this operation. In 1918 he had been the commanding officer of Jagstaffel 56.

Flugkapitän Hans Baur reporting, with his Focke-Wulf Fw 200, to the defender of Demyansk, Generalmajor von Plettenberg (partly obscured).

Demyansk airport after an attack by low flying Soviet aircraft. 266

Hitler's Fw 200 at Demyansk; sixth from right, Generalmajor von Plettenberg.

135

This crew flew the 5000th mission to Demyansk.

Major Beckmann with the same crew of KGr zbV500.
269

Ju 52 N3+IX of KGr zbV172 coming into land at Demyansk.

136

Soviet units tried incessantly to interfere with supply flights for Demyansk with their Stormovik aircraft.

Another Ju 52 destroyed by the Soviets at Demyansk.

Supplies for Kholm. Conditions here were even less favourable than those at Demyansk.

137

Mediterranean and North Africa 1942

On 21 January 1942 General Rommel once again took the initiative on the North Africa Front. Panzergruppe Afrika broke out of the Marada-Marsa-el-Brega position, overran the forces of the 30th British Corps near Agedabia and captured Benghazi on 28 January. The advance then continued in the direction of Derna, but came to a halt on 7 February near El-Gazala, west of Tobruk. The air transport units had been given the order to fly, with all serviceable Ju 52s, aircraft fuel from Benghazi to Matuba. From there it was taken by 25 Ju 52s twice daily via Crete to Derna. In effect, this was a waste of fuel. A Ju 52 needed 2400 litres of fuel for the return flight from Maleme (Crete) to Tobruk and as much as 3200 litres for the trip to Benghazi. Since the fuel tanks of the planes were not sufficiently large for the return flight, part of the fuel brought to the new site had to be used for the return journey. This meant that only 2000 litres of fuel remained for the North Africa Corps after a flight to Tobruk, and only 1200 litres after a delivery to Benghazi. 6000 litres of fuel were needed to take 18 soldiers from Brindisi via Maleme to Tobruk, and 3800 litres for the trip from Athens to Tobruk. Since fighter protection for the Ju 52s was rarely available, the planes had to rely on their own defence. This worked reasonably well until the beginning of May, since 2nd Fliegerkorps constantly attacked Malta and the British fighters there were kept busy. Meanwhile, KGr zbV400 had arrived at Brindisi and flew personnel to Crete, who were then taken on to Derna. A catastrophe occurred on 12 May, when 13 Ju 52s encountered British fighter planes north of Derna. Eight Ju 52s were hit and came down in flames, one landed, badly damaged by gun fire, on the beach at Derna, while the remaining four, which were also damaged, actually landed at Derna. Result: 13 Ju 52s eliminated, 175 soldiers killed, 40 men rescued by sea rescue planes.

From now on routes and flight times were once again changed regularly. Whenever available, Bf 109s of JG27 were made available to meet the Ju 52 units before they reached the coast north of Derna. The operational availability of the Ju 52 units decreased all the time; this was due to aircraft being shot down, or becoming unfit for service of a lack of spare parts. In order to meet the requirements of the different army units, at least in part, the crews flew three missions every day with a total flying time of 12 hours. On 21 May Hitler took, yet again, one of his many wrong decisions of 1942: operation 'Hercules', the occupation of Malta, was postponed indefinitely despite protests by the Italians, who clearly recognized the importance of neutralizing Malta, if supplies to North Africa were to be maintained. On 26 May operation 'Theseus' started, Rommel's new offensive on the El-Gazala Front; initially this was unable to proceed beyond the desert position of Bir-Hacheim, defended by the 1st Free-French Brigade. In Germany, the first 1000-bomber attack on Cologne, during the night 30/31 May 1942, indicated what the Reich could expect from constantly intensified air raids by the Allied Forces. On 10 June Bir-Hacheim fell, and on 21 June Tobruk followed. One day later Hitler appointed Rommel Generalfeldmarschall. In order to ensure the further advance of German forces in the direction of Egypt/Suez Canal, IV/KG zbV1 and KGr zbV600 and 800 were moved to the Mediterranean. Since Luftlandegeschwager (LLG) 1 (Airborne Group) was also temporarily used to provide transport services, it became possible to meet the request by Panzer-Armee Afrika for a daily 1000 men and 25 tonnes of supplies. Between 10 February and 30 June 1942, the transport units, exclusively using Ju 52s carried 28,200 soldiers and 4400 tonnes of fuel and ammunition from Crete to Africa in 4425 missions. On the return flights 10,700 wounded and soldiers due for leave were carried. These missions required 300,000 litres of fuel per day. On 30 June El Alamein was reached. At the same time the German and Italian forces had reached the end of their capability. Rommel had only 70 tanks left and found himself 100 km west of Alexandria. For three days, the German forces attempted to force their way through the position of the British 8th Army; after that Rommel broke off the offensive. On 16 July the British, in turn, tried to advance towards the west, but they had to abandon the attempt on 27 July. In the middle of August the British succeeded in reaching Malta with convoy 'Pedestal'. From now on the British forces were in a position to interfere seriously, from Malta, with the supply routes to North Africa. The Chief of Air Transport in the Mediterranean now had the following units at his disposal:

II/KG zbV1 at Tobruk
IV/KG zbV1 at Maleme
KGr zbV400 at Brindisi
KGr zbV600 at Brindisi
KGr zbV800 at Brindisi
I/LLG in Athens

These units provided daily supplies and reinforcements of about 850 paratroops, flak and army units for the Panzer-Armee Afrika. It was remarkable that hardly any problems with air transport arose between August and October 1942. The reason for this apparent invulnerability was the preparations for the offensive by the British 8th Army near El Alamein, which started on 23 October, and the 'Operation Torch', scheduled for 8 November, by which the Allied Forces planned to land at the rear of the German and Italian lines in Tunisia and Algeria. After the British offensive started on 23 October and led, on 2 November, to a breakthrough of the German lines, the British fighters were able to advance their positions. Accordingly, the Ju 52s, most of which still flew without fighter protection, suffered increasing losses. By mid-November their numbers had been reduced to between 50 and 60. Despite increasingly difficult conditions, by 19 November 1942, they had succeeded in transporting 42,000 soldiers and around 15,000 tonnes of supplies of all kinds to Africa, and in carrying on their return flights 9000 sick and wounded in 11,500 missions. After the landings in Tunisia and Algeria, Chief of Transport for the Mediterranean, Generalmajor Buchholz, had to regroup his Ju 52 units. The only remaining groups were 'S' (Sicily) and 'N' (Naples). 'Operation Torch' started on 8 November. On the following day the airstrip of El Aouina was occupied by German troops, and the day after that the one at Sidi Ahmed near Bizerta. On 17 November the first encounter with Allied units took place 50 km west of Bizerta. The transport planes, initially only Ju 52s, but later also the large Messerschmitt Me 323 transport aircraft, had to supply the bridgehead in Tunis and the units of Luftwaffe in the Tripoli-Gabes area. During the day the machines flew in formation of about 100 aircraft. The flow of transport aircraft extended over the entire distance from Trapani to Tunis as far as Cap Bon. Protection by fighter aircraft was provided in each case by three Bf 109s or Bf 110s. During the night the machines flew singly at ten minute intervals but British Beaufighter night fighters caused considerable losses. Although the unit included large numbers of experienced transport pilots, they also incorporated KGr zbV7 and 11, crews that had been haphazardly put together from a wide variety of units and training schools; their lack of practical experience led to unusually high losses. Nevertheless, morale remained high, but at the height of this hopeless situation an urgent order arrived that as many air transport units as possible should be withdrawn from the Mediterranean front. Only 200 Ju 52s, 15 Me 323s, and a small number of Italian Fiat G 12s and Savoia SM 82s remained for the supply flights to Tunisia and Lybia. What had happened?

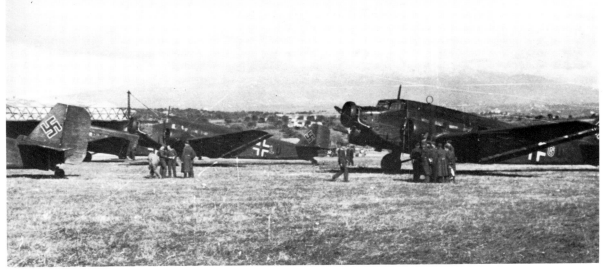

Ju 52 of KGr zbV400 at Brindisi.

Ju 52 of 11/KG zbV1 at Derna.

Air squadron Ju 52 landing at Derna.

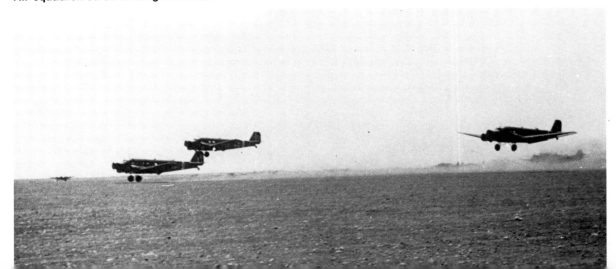

Indefatigable Ju 52s cross the Mediterranean.

By flying in close formation the Ju 52s covered each other.

Again and again KG zbV flew fuel and ammunition to Africa.

Top: the original of this photograph showing transport planes was also damaged.

Middle: even the brand new Ju 252V4 was used for supply flights to Africa. This is Benghazi airport.

Right: General major Seidemann was the last 'Fliegerführer Africa' to continue the hopeless fight against Anglo-American superiority.

Ju 52 of 8/KG zbV1 flying soldiers from Sicily to Tunis.

Ju 52-3mg8e of the seaplane transport squadron at Orbetello.

Fitted with floats the Ju 52 proved to be particularly useful in the Aegean.

143

American North American B-25Cs caught a German squadron on the way to Tunisia and shot down a number of Ju 52s.

This is Ju 52, CE + KN, belonging to the transport squadron of II Fliegerkorps, remained in Cyrenaika after the retreat.

Gotha Go 242 transport gliders were also used for supply flights in Africa. This is a view from a Go 242 to the towing aircraft.

144

This photograph, taken by an American crew, is of a Ju 52 with DFS 230 shortly before it was shot down by the American machine.

Stalingrad 22 November to 2 February 1943

On 19 November 1942 at 0500 hours two Soviet army groups, 'South West Front' and 'Don Front' started a large-scale attack and broke through the lines of the Romanian 3rd Army. One day later the offensive of the 3rd Army Group, the 'Stalingrad Front' took place south of Stalingrad. It was a two-pronged attack, similar to that carried out at Demyansk, but on a much larger scale. Within 48 hours the ring had been closed around the 6th Army, the 4th Army Corps, the 20th Romanian Infantry Division, and the 1st Romanian Cavalry Division. Around 250,000 men were trapped. Hitler's only reaction was the order: 'The 6th Army will form a hedgehog-defence and wait for relief from the outside'.

All responsible commanders of the Luftwaffe units agreed that it would be impossible to supply the 6th Army in the same way as at Demyansk. The chief-of-staff of the 6th Army, Generalmajor Arthur Schmidt, on the other hand, stated as late as 21 November 1942: 'Supplies can be brought in by air'. According to statements made by the general chiefs-of-staff of the air force and the army, Generaloberst Jeschonnek and Generaloberst Zeitzler, Göring confirmed to Hitler that the 6th Army would be supplied by the Luftwaffe. Göring's closest confidant, Generaloberst Bruno Loerzer, reported after the war that Göring had told him: 'Hitler grabbed me: 'Listen, Göring, if the Luftwaffe cannot supply the 6th Army then the whole Army is lost''. After this I could do nothing but agree; otherwise I and the Luftwaffe would have been blamed from the beginning. I simply had to say "Jawohl, mein Führer, we will manage!" ' This meant the death sentence not only for the 6th Army but for hundreds of Ju 52s and other crews. The further events of the Battle of Stalingrad, which marked the turning point for Germany, have been described so often that they need not be repeated here. Only the fate of the Ju 52s and

their crews during this battle will be dealt with.

In the area of Luftflotte 4, the Luftwaffe units responsible for the army Groups A (Caucasus) and B (Stalingrad) the following Ju 52 units were available: the staff of KG zbV1 (Oberst Förster) and the combat units zbV 50, 102, 172, and 900, also KGr zbV5, equipped with He 111s. Air supplies were also flown by KG27 and 55 as well as II/KG4, all equipped with He 111Hs. The total operational strength of these units, all of which had been in constant action since summer 1942, was only about 40 per cent of the target strength! The following additional units were made available, by the beginning of December 1942, for supplying Stalingrad through the air: KGr zbV9, 105, 500, 700, 900 and groups I and II of KG zbv1, all equipped with Ju 52s. Also involved were 14 units with 14 other types of aircraft (He 111, Ju 86, He 177, Fw 200, Ju 90, and Ju 290). General Fiebig was given the overall command for supplying Stalingrad by air. Oberst Förster, Kommodore of KG zbV1 took command of air transport units which had been assembled at Tasinskaya airfield. The four-engine large capacity aircraft were stationed at Stalino. The He 111 units were stationed at Moroskovskaya and were under the command of Oberst Kühl, while Major Willers was responsible for the four-engine planes at Stalino. The constantly changing, and always poor, weather conditions presented the transport pilots with continual problems. In the encircled pocket Pityomnik airfield was under constant surveillance by Soviet fighter planes, which were particularly successful in causing considerable losses among the Ju 52s during take-off and landing. Further losses occurred through shell and artillery fire as well as strafing aircraft. On 18 January 1943 alone, 30 Ju 52s were damaged, ten of these being total losses. The fact that the Soviet fighter planes did not fly regular missions

146

was of some consolation, otherwise the Soviets would no doubt have succeeded in stopping the airlift at an early stage.

During the period 25 November 1942 – 11 January 1943, 5227 tonnes of supplies were flown to Stalingrad. After that date the Soviets captured Pityomnik, so supplies could only be parachuted. During the last phase, until 2 February 1943, the day of the capitulation, a further 1169 tonnes of supplies were dropped, but of this, at least 50 per cent was lost. If one considers that of the 488 aircraft lost during the Stalingrad airlift, 266 alone were Ju 52s, it becomes apparent how, for the second time since their operation in Holland in 1940, the air transport units were significantly reduced. Even more damaging were the losses of flying crew. These losses amounted to about 1000 men, among them many old and experienced pilots, including Flugkapitän Haenig of Lufthansa, who crashed in a Ju 290. The losses were not only due to enemy action but also to the extreme weather conditions. Pityomnik airfield was fully equipped for day and night flights, but the small airfields of Bassargino, Gumrak, Karpovka, and Stalingradsky were suitable only for limited use by day and not at all at night. Tatsinskaya airfield was under fire from 24 December 1942 onward and had to be rapidly evacuated. General Fiebig intended to evacuate on 23 December, but was forbidden to do so by Göring's express personal order. When Fiebig, on his own responsibility, gave the order to take off on Christmas Eve, the ensuing hasty action led to chaos: 109 Ju 52s were able to escape, while 55 were lost. The Ju 52 units lost crews totalling around 250 men. The air transport units were never able to recover from these losses. In January 1943 the first Ju 252 was handed over to the air transport squadron LTS 290. After about a dozen Ju 252s had been built, production ceased because of raw material shortages. Instead, Ju 352, a mixed materials aircraft, was developed.

Ju 52-3mg4e of
KGr zbV400.

Ju 52 of KGr zbV500
at Kirovograd
before its start to
Tatsinskaya.

The ground crew
sank up to their
knees into the
snow.

Ju 52 engines being preheated. Without these preparations the engines would not start.

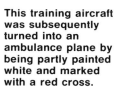

This training aircraft was subsequently turned into an ambulance plane by being partly painted white and marked with a red cross.

Ju 52 taking off for Stalingrad.

149

Ju 52 of KG zbV1 on its flight back from Stalingrad.

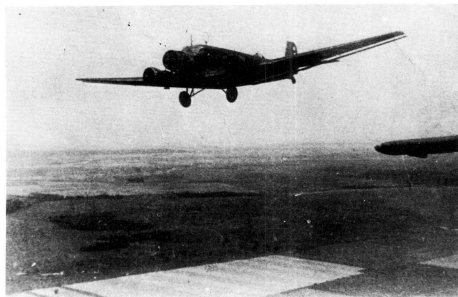

The rapid changes in weather necessitated changes in altitude.

A solid cover of cloud provided protection against Soviet anti-aircraft guns but not against fighter planes.

150

Ju 52-3mg8e 9G+KW of KGr zbV101 on its way to Pitomnik.

Very often the 7.9 mm MG15 was replaced by a 12.7 mm MG131.

Because of the terrifyingly high losses the ambulance planes were kept busy.

The unfavourable landing
conditions resulted more
and more frequently in
crash-landings.

An old Lufthansa Ju 52-
3mge, BT + AY, was used
by army staff as a transport
aircraft.

Crash-landing at Tat-
sinskaya as a result of anti-
aircraft fire.

This sort of clear weather was extremely rare during the Stalingrad operation.

Unloading a Ju 52 at Pitomnik.

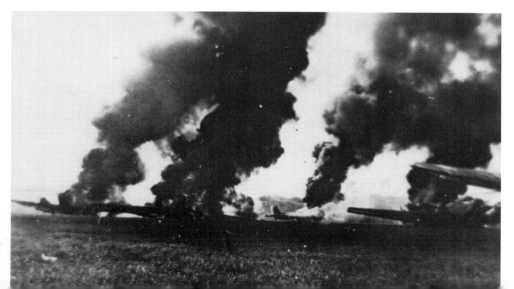

Five Ju 52s on fire after an attack by a Soviet Stormovik.

153

Soviet Stormovik aircraft repeatedly succeeded in surprising transport at Pitomnik, destroying many of them.

Many aircraft crash-landed as a result of attacks during landing.

Crash-landing after an air battle at Tatsinskaya.

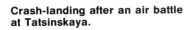

154

Flying operations nevertheless continued, even with an old Ju 52-3mge from a flying school.

From the middle of January 1943 onward, supplies could only be parachuted into Stalingrad, since Pitomnik airport had been taken by the Soviets.

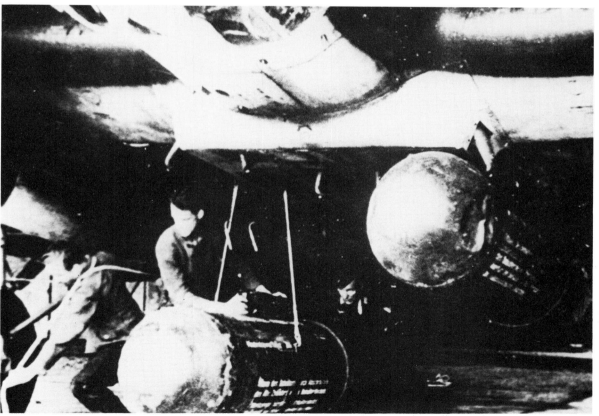

1943 –
reorganisation of the air transport units

The situation in North Africa had become hopeless. Rommel's last attempt at an offensive against the British 8th Army had been in vain. In the East, Soviet armies forced the German units back at an increasing pace, and at home air warfare above the territory of the Reich impeded the efforts of the German armaments industry. Losses of transport aircraft rose from week to week. On 5 April US fighter planes attacked a JU 52 unit near Cap Bon and shot down 14 Ju 52s, who had to fly without the protection of fighter planes. US bombers attacked transport aircraft bases in Sicily and destroyed ten Ju 52s, while a further 65 were damaged. On 18 April American fighter pilots shot down 24 Ju 52s out of 65, despite fighter plane protection by 16 Bf 109s and five Bf 110s, while a further 35 were so badly damaged that they had to make emergency landings and fell into enemy hands. On 13 May 1943 the tragedy in North Africa was over. The transport planes, Ju 52s and Me 323s, had flown 8388 soldiers and 5040 tonnes of supplies to North Africa; 76 Ju 52s and 14 Me 323s had been shot down and 275 crew members had been killed or wounded.

On 15 May 1943 the air transport units were reorganised. They were combined to form 14th Fliegerkorps with headquarters at Tutow, Pomerania. The staff of Lufttransportführer was disbanded and turned into the staff of Lufttransportfliegerführer 1. Generalmajor Morzig was appointed head of the eastern section, while Generalmajor Buchholz became responsible for the Mediterranean. KG zbv and KGr zbv no longer existed afterwards. Instead, Transportgeschwader (TG) 1 – 4, using Ju 52s, and TG5, using two groups of Me 323s, were formed. TG 1 – 4, each consisted of four Transport Gruppen (TGr), each with a flight of five Ju 52s and four

squadrons of 12 Ju 52s each. A TGr thus consisted of 53 Ju 52s. This target strength was, however, rarely achieved. This arrangement remained in force until the end of the war, although the TG and TGr continued to decrease in numbers as a result of fuel shortages and insufficient supplies of aircraft. In line with the other generals, General der Flieger Coeler was appointed General der Transportflieger.

During 1943 three further versions of Ju 52 were developed:

JU 52-3mg10e, optionally with wheel or float landing gear. Armed with a MG 13 and two further MG 15s, otherwise similar to g9e; this was built at Amiot in France; BMW 132Z engine.

Ju 52-3mg12e troop transporter with BMW 132L. Only a small number were built, some of which went to Lufthansa.

JU 52-3mg14e land and sea transport plane, similar to g8e; increased armour plating to protect the pilot; only a small number float planes. Increased lateral armament.

Transport pilots now used aircraft wherever they could find them. Even Italian and French models flew for the TGr. Four Ju 52s, supplied in 1935 to the Italian air line Ala Littoria (I-BIZI, I-BIOS, I-BOAN, and I-BERO) now flew as AI + AO (works number 4064), AS + PI (works number 6710), AI + AT (works number unknown), and AS + PE (works number 6803). The Ju units belonging to Luftflotte 5 had been badly mauled: on 10 January 1943 Ju 52s of the 4/KGr zbv108 and four ambulance Ju 52s of the ambulance squadron were at the Finnish airport of Kemi, and one courier Ju 52 as well as five transport Ju

52s of the transport squadron 'Norway' at Rovaniemi. In July 1943 the number of aircraft at Finnish airports was as follows:

At Kemi 12 Ju 52 of 4/TrGr 20 and 3 Ju 52 for ambulance duties, and at Rovaniemi 5 Ju 52 of the 'Norway' transport squadron. After the end of the Stalingrad missions air supplies to the 17th Army at the Kuban bridgehead began on 4 February 1943. In addition to the Ju 52/transport glider groups came KGr zbv9, 50, 102, 172, and 500, which had previously been in action at Demyansk and Stalingrad, all equipped with JU 52 but by no means in full strength, although I and II KG zbv1 and KGr zbv 700 and 900 had had to transfer to them personnel, aircraft and equipment. Bases for the Kuban bridgehead were initially Taganrog, Stalino, and Zaporoshye. They were then moved to the Crimea.

During a supply period of seven weeks 5418 tonnes of supplies were flown to the Kuban bridgehead, which corresponds to 182 tonnes daily. The actual strength of the Ju 52 units was 40 to 45 aircraft. On average 30 Ju 52s flew missions each day. To this total must be added the transport gliders, which also made a considerable contribution to the supply effort. Since this airlift operation entailed considerably fewer difficulties than did the Stalingrad operation it ran quite smoothly. During the last phase of evacuating the Kuban bridgehead, between 7 September and 9 October, transport and towing units moved 15,661 soldiers and 1154 tonnes of equipment to the Crimea.

After the end of October 1942 work was in progress on the Ju 352. Apart from the freight hatch, no components of the Ju 52 were used, since the design was an entirely new one and entailed composite construction methods. Production of the Jumo 211F and J engines had been affected, as a result of continuous air attacks, to such an extent that output met only just under half the requirements for Ju 88s and He 111Hs, and the BMW-Bramo 323R-2 was to be used instead. The fuselage consisted of a tubular steel structure, covered partly with plywood and partly with fabric. The cockpit canopy was the same as that of the Ju 290. The wing took the form of a wooden structure in three sections. The landing gear had been simplified compared with that of the Ju 252. Since Junkers had no available capacity because of the workload for the Ju 88/188 programme, construction work on the Ju 352 started at the Fritzlar airbase. The first aircraft Ju 352 V1, took off on its maiden flight on 1 October 1943. This and the second prototype, Ju 352 V2, were unarmed. Like the Ju 52, the JU 352 also had only one MG position, at the rear of the fuselage, but was equipped for its defence with an MG151/20 instead of the MG131. In order to reduce the landing distance, the Ju 352 was the first German aircraft to be fitted with fully reversible propellers, designed by Messerschmitt and built by Vereinigte Deutsche Metallwerke (VDM). At the end of 1943 the first three Ju 352s were still undergoing trials.

Despite the described shortfalls in the supply capacity of Ju 52-3m's, Germany was forced, for political and economic reasons, to export these aircraft. Under a trade agreement concluded in 1943 between Germany and Turkey, for example, it was stipulated that five Ju 52-3m's should be supplied to that country. These machines were partly intended for the most important Turkish air route, Istanbul – Ankara – Adana. At the same time Turkey was involved in negotiations with Romania on the establishment of an air link between Bucharest and Istanbul, in which both sides were to use the Ju 52-3m. The war prevented the realization of this project.

Ju 52-3mg10e of the transportgeschwader (TG)3.

Ju 52-3mg6e of the 8th Squadron of
II/TG4.

Flights continued, although the allied forces largely dominated the
airspace above Germany.

The former I-BIZI of Ala Lottoria was used by the Luftwaffe as a transport plane under the designation AI+AC.

Finland: General Dietl (third from right) with his official machine at JG5.

One of the three ambulance Ju 52s of the ambulance service Luftflotte 5.

159

Ambulance Ju 52 in Karelia with SS Mountain Division 'North'.

Ju 52-3mg6e PI+OA of the chief of Technical Services of Luftflotte 5, Flieger-Oberstabsingenieur R. Scholz.

In service until the bitter end, 1944/45

The beginning of 1944 saw, in addition to a constant intensification of Allied air attacks, the large-scale attack by the Soviets on the German Heeresgruppe Nord in mid-January. One week later the US 5th Army landed in the Anzio and Netuno area, south of Rome. On 27 January 1944 the Soviet attack started on the weak northern wing of the German Heeresgruppe Süd. From now on the increasingly weak German armies were repeatedly flanked and their lines penetrated. The transport units with their old Ju 52s had to supply the enclosed or isolated units to enable their retreat or break-out. On 28 January the first supplies were sent on their way to the 8th Army, which was surrounded near Cherkassy, an operation in which the II/TG3, III/TG3 and I/TG1 were involved. From 16 February 1944 onward no further air supplies were needed, since the link-up with the relief unit had been established. The three groups flew about 1500 missions, taking 2026 tonnes of supplies to the encircled area. On their return journeys 700 heavily wounded and 1700 minor casualties were flown back. Thirty-two Ju 52s were lost during this action; 113 were damaged but were always put back into operation by ground staff working day and night.

On 1 November 1943 the 4th Ukrainian Front of the Soviet side entirely cut off the 17th German Army in the Crimea from its supply routes to the mainland. Under the command of Generalmajor Morzik and his staff an airlift was set up to supply the 17th Army. The following Ju 52 units were involved: TG2 with I and III Groups, TG3 with II and III Groups and I/TG4. Supply flights to the units in the Crimea continued until the final evacuation on 11 May 1944. No exact figures are available on performance and losses during this operation.

In mid-March 1944 the 1st Panzer Army was cut off in the area of Kamenets-Podolsk. Here, too, air supplies were carried out under the command of Generalmajor Morzig, who, for this purpose had been put in charge of the following Ju 52 units: I/TG1, I/TG3, I/TG4, and IV/TG1. In addition, some He 111 units had been allocated, which started dropping supplies as early as 26 March. The Ju 52s were all loaded at Lemberg. It was possible to discontinue supplies on 10 April 1944. On 1 May 1944 the total number of Ju 52 units was 14 groups and independent squadrons: in all about 500 - 600 52s which were by no means all fit for operation.

On 6 June 1944 the invasion by the Allied Forces started in Normandy. Once the Amiot works at Colombes near Paris had been occupied, no further Ju 52s were supplied to the Luftwaffe. These were the last works to be building the Ju 52. Within the territory of the Reich no Ju 52 production existed. Only at Fritzlar were Ju 352s still being made; but these hardly saw active service. This also meant that the activities of Ju 52MSs in France came to an end, after they had to stop operations in the Black Sea area after the Crimea had been re-taken. The larger part of these mine detector units were moved to the Baltic and some to Budapest, where they fought in vain against the aircraft of 205 Squadron of the Royal Air Force, which each night placed new mines in the Danube and thus severely interfered with fuel transports from Hungary and Romania. The Ju 52MSs were allocated an operating range from Vienna via Belgrade as far as the Iron Gate – on the Danube. Early in 1944 three Ju 52MSs had been moved to Finland, where they cleared mines in the Gulf of Finland. The 'Mausis' remaining on the Danube were moved to Pomerania in late autumn, where a number of mine destroying missions were flown to cover the retreat from East Prussia. Until the end of 1944 'Mausis' still flew missions along the coast between the mouths of the Elbe and Weser rivers until lack of fuel forced them to stop their operations. The picture in the Baltic was different: as late as 10 February 1945 the following telex was sent from the Command of the Luftwaffe to Luftflotte 6 and Luftflotte Reich: 'Because of intensified mine laying in the Belt and Baltic increase mine detection and removal operations with Ju 52s in Liaison with MOK (Supreme Command Marine) East. Fuel from air fleet supplies. No special allocations.' This last sentence illustrates impressively how bad were fuel supplies for the army.

On 20 December 1944, 33,000 German and 37,000 Hungarian soldiers as well as the civilian population were surrounded in Budapest. Relief operations failed. It was impossible to supply troops and civilians from the air but, nevertheless Generalleutnant Conrad was ordered to solve this insoluble problem, in an operation which was to be carried out with TGr III of TG2 and TG3, I/LLG2 and a Hungarian Ju 52 squadron. Everybody realized that this attempt was insufficiently equipped and doomed to fail from the beginning. On 11 February the last defenders of Budapest were overpowered. After an attempted break-out only 785 men succeeded in reaching the German lines. Of the 64 Ju 52s used for this operation 52 and their crews were lost.

The greatest supply operation by transport aircraft during the last months of the war both in terms of scope and losses, was the supply of Breslau, which was encircled on 15 February 1945. No figures are available on the activity of transport planes during the supply of Breslau, but it is known that 165 transport aircraft, mainly Ju 52s, and their crews were lost. During the night of 6/7 April the last three Ju 52s landed in the beseiged city and took with them on their return flight 52 wounded, and 2 air crew. Once the airports south of Berlin had fallen into enemy hands, supply flights to Breslau became almost impossible. During the night of 1 May 1945, seven Ju 52s once again dropped supplies

above the city. Two Fiesler Fi 156 Storch landed and collected transport glider crews. On 6 May Breslau capitulated.

A difficult, but in the end successful, supply operation concerned the supply of the Panzer groups 'Nehring' and 'Saucken', which made their way back from Poland and East Prussia. This entailed supplying with fuel and ammunition a unit which was encircled but at the same time moved west. During the night of 21 January 1945 He 111Hs dropped 82 supply containers, each with 250 kg of tank ammunition and fuel, in the Petrikau area. During the night of 29 January 24 Ju 52s of an initial 27 landed near the 24th Panzerkorps, unloaded 48,000 litres of fuel and returned with 206 wounded. During the course of the next day the units reached the left bank of the Oder. The greater part of the German units was saved, which would not have been possible without air supplies. The events near Posen, where 12,000 men had been encircled, took a similar turn to those of Breslau. 195 Ju 52s and He 111Hs had been allocated to carry out supply flights; of these 169 completed their mission, and flew 257.08 tonnes of supplies to Posen; although after 8 February it was no longer possible to land but only to parachute supplies. On 23 February 1945 the drama of Posen came to an end. A similar fate seemed to be in store for Schneidemuhl. Fortunately Ju 52s were able to land there until the last day of the seige, 13 February 1945, landing 257 tonnes of supplies and returning with 277 persons, among them 237 wounded. 1000 soldiers tried to break out in a westerly direction, but only 184 reached the German lines. 9000 men ended in Soviet captivity. Similar events took place at Arnswalde and Glogau. Having been supplied by air for a week, Arnswalde was relieved by the 11th SS-Panzer Army. The seige of Glogau lasted until 26 March 1945. After that, the fight was over despite supplies from the air.

Only the following units were available during the last months of the Second World War for supply missions:

I/TG1 (JU 52)	Commander: Major Schmidt; location, Tutow	
II/TG2 (JU 52)	Commander: Hauptmann Kurt Harnisch; location, Senftenberg	
III/TG2 (Ju 52)	Commander: Major Reimann; location, Dresden-Klotzsche	
I/TG3 (Ju 52)	Commander: Hauptmann Georg-Dieter Matschullat; location, Senftenberg	
II/TG3 (Ju 52)	Commander: Oberstleutnant Otto Baumann; location, Werder	
III/TG3 (Ju 52)	Commander: Major Penkert; location, Finsterwalde	
TGr30 (He 111)	Commanders: Oberstleutnant Heinz Klamke, Hauptmann Erich Langer; locations: Klein-Welzheim, Reichenbach, Neubiberg, Saltzburg	
Large transporter (Ju 352)	Commander: Major Günter Mauss; location, Tutow	
KG4 (Groups I and III) (He III) (He 111)	Commander: Major Reinhard Graubner; location, Königsgrätz	

On the western Front, transport operations with Ju 52s were virtually impossible during these last months of the war as a result of Allied superiority in the air, especially of their night fighters. During the offensive in the Ardennes on 16 December 1944 a total of 67 Ju 52s of II/TG3 and other transport squadrons under the command of Major Baumann were able to land paratroopers in the Hohe Venn and these were subsequently successfully deployed. This success remained, however, without effect on the total operation.

A last report on available aircraft dated 25 April 1945 provided the following figures:

I/TG1 at Windau/Courland	11 Ju 52s
Squadron Tutow	14 Ju 52s
II/TG1, 3rd squadron, Puttnitz	15 Ju 52Ws
II/TG2 at Schrasslawitz	31 Ju 52s
III/TG2 at Klattau	
I/TG 3 at Neuenburg	24 Ju 52s
II/TG 3 at Güstrow/Mecklenburg	34 Ju 52s
III/TG 3 at Wimsbach	37 Ju 52s
Tr. Gr. 20 in Oslo (Norway)	38 Ju 52s
Sea Transport Squadron 2 at Hommeliok (Norway)	7 Ju 52Ws

This is a total of 190 Ju 52s and 22 Ju 52s with floats. To these came 23 Ju 352s at Totow. It is unlikely that this figure changed much between that date and the capitulation of the Wehrmacht on 7 May 1945. On 20 April 1945 the last plane of Deutsche Lufthansa to leave Berlin was a Ju 52-3m. After a stop-over in Munich the machine flew on. From that day onward both aircraft and crew have been lost without trace, and nothing is known of their fate. After this, the history of the JU 52 should have come to an end. Events were to show, however, that despite its age it was still in demand as a useful transport plane.

This Ju 52 *Max Limbach,* remained at Tempelhof when all other Lufthansa aircraft were removed on 22 April 1945.

The end of January 1945. A Ju 52 on the way with supplies for the German 8th Army, encircled near Cherkassy.

Ju 352VI during final assembly work at Fritzlar.

164

For the first time Ju 352 V1 taxis from the assembly bay.

On 3 May 1944 a Ju 188E-1, works number 260151, collided with Ju 252 V6.

Early 1944. Airlift to the Crimea for the supply and later evacuation of the German 17th Army.

Spring 1944. Air supply of the 1st Panzer Army, encircled near Kamenets-Podolsk, with Ju 52 von Lemberg.

Ju 52MS in France before it was moved to the Baltic.

Ju 52MS in readiness on the Baltic coast.

Generalleutnant Conrad was given the order to supply Budapest from the air in December 1944.

Ju 52-3mg4e of the Hungarian air force.

One of the few Ju 52s not to get lost during the Breslau air supply mission.

Lufthansa Ju 52
D-AMFR *Ludwig Hau-*
tzmayer, **works num-
ber 5933, remained in
an allotment near
Berlin-Tempelhof
until 1947.**

**Ju 52-3mg6e of IV/
TG20.**

**JU 52-3mg2e D-AKIY
of Lufthansa, works
number 5429, was at
Horten (Norway) in
1945 and was taken
over by the Norwe-
gians. It remained in
service until Septem-
ber 1945.**

This Ju 52-3mgI4e U-1 DP+FJ, works number 640416, was originally used by the Kriegsmarine as a transport plane for its supreme command. It landed at Bonarp (Sweden) with refugees on May 1945.

Ju 52-3mg8e of TG20 at Kjevik (Norway), Summer 1945.

Coming from Libau, on the Courland front, this Ju 52-3mg10e, JU+BM of IV/TG1, landed on 8 May 1945 at Bulltofta, Sweden, with 32 soldiers on board.

This Ju 52-3m stood at Leck in Holstein, until the winter of 1946.

The French Ju 52 – AAC1 Toucan

As a result of the Wiesbaden Agreement of 23 July 1941 between the Reich and the French Vichy Government 2000 German aircraft were to be built in France. Subsequently the production of Ju 52-3mg10e's started in the former Amiot works at Colombes, just north-west of Paris. At first, the monthly total was 10 machines, but this was soon increased, and by the beginning of the invasion and the occupation of Paris 321 Ju 52s had been delivered to the Luftwaffe. After the French had once agained assumed power, it was decided to continue building Ju 52-3mg10e's without modifications. The works were now called 'Ateliers Aéronautiques de Colombes', and the Ju 52 produced there known as the Ju 52 AAC1. The French Air Force (Armée de l'Air) continued to call it the Ju 52, however. The first eight AAC1s formed the basis for the fleet of the new 'Air France', which used these aircraft for regular flights during the winter of 1944/45. During a period of two years more than 400 AAC1s were built. The last, with the works number 415, joined the Armée de l'Air in 1948. As far as can be ascertained, 216 AAC1s were supplied to the French air force and 12 to the navy. To these were added 38 Ju 52s which were former Luftwaffe machines that had been reconditioned. Three Ju 52s, belonging to the Luftwaffe, were flown from Norwegian airports to France and also incorporated in the Armée de l'Air. The old Ju 52-3-m's with the works numbers 0645, 0703, 1109, and 313558 were also flown for a number of years by the Armée de l'Air. Works number 1009 was the last of the German Ju 52s to be taken from service, in 1956.

Thirteen of the Ju 52 built at Colombes were registered for Air France. Some went later to Air Atlas, Aéro-Cargo, Aigle Azur, Air Nolis, Air Océan, and Compagnie Générale Transsahariennne. One of the machines built at Colombes can today be seen at the Deutsches Museum in Munich. The Ju 52s of the Armée de l'Air were to prove their worth in active service until 1952.

After most of the German troops had moved out of the country France started building its new air force. As early as 1 February 1945 the first transport unit was formed at Le Bourget under the name Groupe de Transport (GT) 3/15, consisting of one squadron of Ju 52 3-m's and one squadron of Douglas C-47s. These units formed the basis for the French air Force's transport section, Groupement des Moyens Militaires de Transport Aérien (GMMTA). GT3/15 'Maine' consisted of former Luftwaffe Ju 52s; its first task was the return to France of French prisoners of war and forced labourers. Subsequently further GTs were formed: on 15 November 1945 GT1/62 'Algérie' in Algiers, in March 1946 in Saigon (Indochina), GT1/34 'Béarn'; and on 1 April 1956 at Bourget and Chartres GT4/15 'Poitou', all equipped with AAC1s. The AAC1s were not without problems: the electrical and radio equipment was partly German, partly French, and partly American. Moreover, the Ju 52 needed a service every 500 hours, in contrast to the C-47, where the servicing interval was only every 1500 hours. Nevertheless Colombes continued to supply Ju 52s to the army, and they were used because not enough other aircraft were available. On 1 July 1947 GMMTA was reorganized and subsequently the following transport units were equipped with Ju 52s:
GT 2/61 'Maine' at Le Bourget, GT 3/16 'Poitou' at Chartres, GT 1/62 'Algérie' at Maison Blanche (Algeria), GT 1/63 'Bretagne' at Mengen (Germany), GT 1/64 'Béarn' at Bien-Hoa (Saigon), and GT 3/64 at Bach-Mai (Indochina).

At the end of March 1947 a revolt occurred in Madagascar. Only three Ju 52s were stationed there, and these were, of course, not sufficient for the speedy transport of reinforcements. GT3/61, equipped with the good old Ju 52

171

brought supplies and paratroopers as soon as possible via El Adem, Khartoum, Nairobi, and Dar-es-Salam. In 1948 a number of Ju 52s of GT2/41 were used during the Berlin airlift. They were stationed at Berlin Tempelhof but were, in fact, rarely used because of their outdated radio equipment. Meanwhile Ho Chi Minh had started attacking French Indochina. On 19 December 1947 the Vietminh simultaneously attacked all French garrisons in Tonkin and Central Annam including those at Hanoi, Bac Ninh, Hon Gai, Lang Son Vinh, Hue and Tourane. The first Ju 52 mission together with a number of C-47s, took place during operation 'Dédale' on 5 and 6 January 1947 after the town of Nam Dinh had been encircled by 5000 Vietminh. Despite intensive artillery fire the French succeeded in dropping a paratroop batallion. Although all the aircraft used for this mission were damaged, they all succeeded in returning to Hanoi. A similar operation was 'Papillon' on 15 April in the area of Hoah Bin, Cho Bo and Moc Han. On 13 May followed operation 'Aphrodite' against Phu To. Between 15 December 1947 and 18 June 1948 the Ju 52s had flown 850 missions, during which 21 aircraft were damaged. A successful operation was the one code-named 'Ondine' on 7 November 1948 during which 20 Ju 52s and six C-47s re-established the link between Hanoi and the North-West Region. The old Ju 52s, which continued to be handicapped by their outdated radio equipment, gradually disappeared from the Indochinese war. By August 1949 only GT2/62 used Ju 52s. These old machines were used for any task that arose: for flying paratroopers, supply flights, bomb attacks — they coped with everything. The Ju 52s flew their last bombing raid on 16 September 1950 at Dong Khé. The last machines were withdrawn from the front in 1952.

The Ju 52 was obsolete as early as 1945. Colonel Chohat, for example, noted in his flight log that the flight from Algiers to Hyères across the Mediterranean took 5 hours 45 minutes. There were caricatures and jokes about the machines, but those who flew them loved them. 'Julie', as it was known to the French crews, was a great favourite. One could 'see something of the countryside', it was reliable and robust. The French General Barthélemy wrote: 'It was in truth the cornerstone of French air transport'.

Of the 415 AAC1s that were built, the Portugese Air Force obtained 13 machines between 2 and 19 December 1960. These were the AAC works numbers 5, 48, 53, 127, 205, 234, 255, 258, 291, 325, 357, 366 and 392. As early as 1957 AAC1, works number 148, went to Portugal where it was registered as CS-ADA. The others were given the military registration numbers 6300 – 6322. The locations of some of them today are:

No. 6301 at the air force base Alverca
No. 6303 at a children's playground at Evora
No. 6304 at a children's playground Coimbra
No. 6311 at Aero Club Viseu
No. 6315 at the air force museum Alverca
No. 6316 at the Imperial War Museum at Duxford
Nr. 6316 at the air force base Ota
A further Portugese Ju 52 is today at the base of the Federal German Luftwaffe at Hohn, Lufttransportgeschwader 63.
A former French AAC1 is at Deutsches Museum in Munich.

AAC1, works number 056, of Air France, in service from February 1945 to February 1953.

This AAC1 flew for the French Air Force until 1955.

AAC1, works number 289, was in service with the French navy until February 1960.

173

This AAC1, destroyed during the Vietnam war, belonged to Group de Transport (GT) 1/34 'Bearn', established in Saigon in 1946.

This crash-landed AAC1, works number 334, also belonged to GT1/34 'Bearn'.

Ju 52s in Spain

Whereas, as was earlier described, the first transport flights of combat troops from Morocco to Spain were carried out in 1936 with German Ju 52s and German crews, the so-called Escuadra B under the command of José Rodrigeuz Diaz de Lecea was ordered to carry out these transports as from August 1936. Escuadra B consisted of three Escuadrillas of three Ju 52s each. These attacked Madrid on 27 and 28 August 1936 which led to difficulties with the German Embassy, since at that time Lufthansa still carried out regular flights to Madrid. One Escuadrilla of Escuadra B formed the core of the first Nationalist bomber squadron Escuadra 4-E-22. The superiority of the Republican fighter aircraft made it necessary to regroup the first Escuadras into night bomber units, 'Grupos de bombardo nocturno'. Two of these groups were formed: 1-G-22 and 2-G-22. Of the 55 Ju 52s supplied by Germany to Franco, 23 serviced the Civil War. These units had flown 13,000 hours during 5400 missions and dropped 6397 tonnes of bombs by March 1939.

The Spanish airline IBERIA had rented three Ju 52-3m's from Lufthansa as early as 1937, and these were later partly bought, with Lufthansa still retaining a 24.5 per cent share which was given up finally in November 1943. By this time IBERIA had seven Ju 52s, their registrations being M-CABA, M-CABB, M-CABC, M-CABU, M-CABE, M-CABO and M-CABY. Three machines were subsequently bought from captured stock of the Allied Forces, and three more from Sweden. The origin of three further machines is uncertain; they may have been machines used for escape from Germany. When the company Construcciones Aeronauticas SA (CASA) started the licensed construction of the Ju 52-3m, known as the CASA 352, they were not used by Iberia, which only flew Ju 52s of German origin. CASA built a total of 170 C 352s, 106 of which were fitted with German BMW 132A engines, the remaining 64 with the improved ENMSA B3 with a performance 90 hp greater than the engines previously used. Both versions were built by Empresa Nacional de Motores de Aviacion SA (formerly Elizalde) in Barcelona. The first CASA 352 made in Spain carried out its maiden flight in June 1945. In 1946/47 Regimento Mixto No.1 was formed at Alcalá de Henares near Madrid; its No. 1 Wing was equipped with CASA 352-Ls, whereas No. 2 Wing used Do 17Es and Hs 123s, left over from the Civil War. In 1951 the last machines of this wing were withdrawn from service and replaced with CASA 352-L; subsequently the entire unit was renamed 'Regimento de Transporte No. 1, continuing in existence in this form until 1955. In July 1955 the unit was moved to Getafe (Madrid) and renamed Ala de Transporte No. 35. From 1956 onward the unit was gradually equipped with Douglas C-47. With the introduction of the first Douglas C-54 the last CASA 352-Ls were removed to other units.

In 1957 Ala de Transport No. 36 was formed at Gando, Canary Islands, with an Escuadron C 352-L. In 1958 this unit was renamed Ala Mixta No. 36 and enlarged by the addition of one Escuadron of North American T-6s, and a third with C-2111s (licence-built versions of the Heinkel He 111). The first squadron was now called 361 Escuadron. On 1 April 1965 the entire unit was renamed Ala Mixta No. 46. The 361 Escuadron retained CASA 352-Ls until 1970/71 when they were replaced by Douglas C-47s. Further CASA 352-Ls flew for Escuela de Polimotores, established in 1951, which was at Jerez de la Frontera until 1965; even an old Ju 52-3m from the time of the Civil War was in operation there. In 1965 the old three-engine planes were replaced by Douglas C-47s.

In August 1947 a paratrooper school (Escuela de Paracaidistas) was founded at Alcantarilla

175

near Murcia. From 1948 onwards C 352-Ls were used there, and they remained in service until 1971/72. A C 352-L, T.2B-181, however, flew until 1978. It is now at Alcantarilla as a memorial.

Further units that used C 352-Ls were:
The Advanced Flying School (Escueda Superior de Vuelo) at Matacán, the Flying School (Academia General del Aire) at San Javier, Escuadrón Cartográfico y Fotografico at Cuatro Vientos near Madrid, Escuadrones des Estado Mayor Nos. 90 and 96 at Getafe, Grupo de Experimentacion en vuelo (test flying units), Inta-Torrejón near Madrid, and finally the liaison unit No. 402 at Tablada near Seville.

The Spanish Air Force is thus shown to have flown almost exclusively CASA 352s or 352-Ls, while the transport aircraft of the Spanish airline Iberia listed below were exclusively Ju 52-3m's built in Germany:

EC-AAF ex D-AUJA		works number 5851
EC-AAG ex D-AXUT		works number 5022
EC-AAH ex D-AKYS		works number 5098
EC-AAI ex D-AGFD ex ZS-AFC		works number 4060
EC-AAJ ex D-AVUL		works number 4073
EC-AAK ex D-AJAT ex OE-LAK		works number 4076
EC-AAL ex D-		works number 7017
EC-AAU ex EC-CAL		works number 6725
EC-ABD ex EC-CAJ		works number 7053
EC-ABE ex EC-CAK		works number 7196
EC-ABF ex EC-CAN		works number 7220
EC-ABR ex EC-DAM		works number 5386
EC-ABS ex EC-DAN		works number 6015
EC-ADO ex SE-AFB		works number 5620
EX-ADP ex SE-AFD		works number 5646
EC-ADQ ex SE-AFC		works number 5633

The first Ju 52 of the Spanish line Iberia, was the former D-AUJA of Lufthansa, works number 5851. It was given the registration EC-AAF and named *Ebro*.

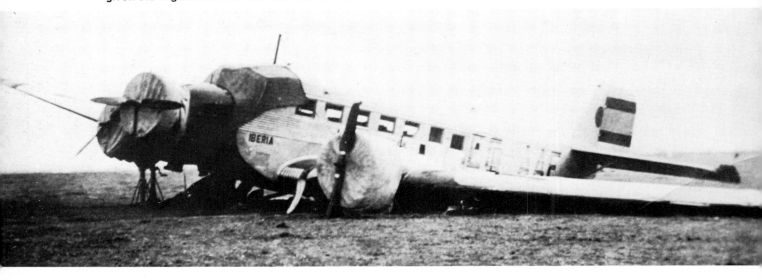

This Ju-3m was built in Germany and belonged to the Grupo de bombardo notturno I-G 22. On its fuselage are the markings of the Falange.

One of the first CASA 352Ls built in Spain.

This CASA 352L was sold to Britain.

Old and modern times meet: Concorde and a CASA 352L.

Ju 52s after 1945

A document issued by the US Air Force dated 7 July 1945 reported on how many Ju 52s were found by the Allied Forces after the end of the war. These were;

On former Reich territory	100 Ju 52s
In Denmark	39 Ju 52s
In Norway	40 Ju 52s
In Belgium	1 Ju 52s

Of this total of 180 machines 43 were destroyed so that 137 Ju 52s were serviceable. Of these, 56 were transferred to Britain, France received 36, of which 27 had landing gear and nine floats, while Denmark received three, Norway 18, Belgium five, Holland four, and Czechoslovakia three. In all, 134 Ju 52s were distributed. The fate of the remaining three is unknown.

In 1939, one month after the outbreak of the war, Junkers had supplied to Switzerland three so-called 'Hörsaalflugzeuge' (flying lecture rooms) Ju 52-3m g4e's, works numbers 6580, 6595, and 6610. They were delivered to Dubendorf, Hangar 9, where they remain today. They were primarily used for training observers and aircraft radio operators, but also carried out some transport operations. During the winter of 1950/51 they proved their worth during supply flights to mountainous regions cut off by avalanches. In 1956 they flew, at the request of the Red Cross, supplies to Hungary. In 1951 they underwent their first major overhaul. Aircraft A-702 was painted in the colours of the Wehrmacht in 1958 when it was used in a film. A-703 collided in 1965 with the radar installation at Dubendorf and had to be fitted with a new wing tip on the left-hand side. Finally, all three were once again used for training the first Swiss paratroopers. After 43 years of service they were finally withdrawn in 1981. The Swiss loved their old Ju 52s and saved them from the scrap yard by founding a 'Save the Ju 52' action group. As a result A-701 and A-703 still carry out pleasure trips, and A-702, which was grounded for some time, has been restored and is now flying again.

Of the four Ju 52s that were sent to the Netherlands one was used for spare parts, while the remaining three formed the basis of the new Dutch Rijksluichtvaart-school. Although, after the period of occupation, the feelings of the Dutch towards Germany were far from warm, the three machines were given the friendliest possible nicknames. Works number 5715, built in 1936 at Weserflug, had been given the number VM985 by the British and was now given the Dutch markings PH-UBA and the name 'Opa' (Grandpa), which was even painted on the fuselage, just behind the engine. Works number 3428, built in 1943 at ATG, had been used after 1945 with the British markings VM927, flown by German civilian crews on mine detection operations off the Dutch coast, now became PH-UUB with the name 'Ome Keesj' (Uncle Cheese). Its exact type designation was Ju-52-3mg8e/MS. The third machine was a Ju 52-3mg10e, built at Amiot under German supervision, with the works number 05210078 which became, after a brief stay with the Royal Air Force as VN743, PH-UBC with the name 'Oma' (Grandma). After a number of years in service with the Rijksluichvaartschool it was eventually taken out of service because of a lack of spare parts.

A similar fate was that of the five Ju 52s handed over to the Belgian Air Force. One was used for spare parts, and the remaining four flew in the sevice of the Belgian Air Force as training and transport planes until they had to be taken out of service for lack of spares.

A report on the fate of the Ju 52s in Spain, and the Ju 52s built in France, which subsequently saw long active service, has already been given.

One Spanish Ju52-3m is in Berlin undergoing restoration work. It is to be exhibited at the new transport museum. The cockpit of the Swedish SE-ADR, works number 4017, is at the Arlanda Museum at Stockholm-Bromma airport.

A particularly well preserved machine, still in flying order, is Casa 352, which was restored from October 1983 onwards at Rochester (England). The machine was painted in the correct Luftwaffe colours being given the markings 1Z + EK of the 2nd squadron of I group of KG zbV1. In contrast to the Ju 52-3m's displayed in Germany this machine is painted with swastika and the characteristic black cross, outlined in white, without anybody in Britain objecting. The Ju 52s given to Britain in 1945 were given the Royal Air Force serial numbers VM892, VM900-932, VM961-989, VN176-177, VN709-731, and VN740-756. It would appear that not all these machines actually went to the Royal Air Force. Ten were given to British European Airways and were used on routes to and from the British Isles. Three Ju 52s went to the British Air Ministry where they were given the registration numbers Air Min 102-104. Air Min 104 was works number 5375, which had been flown on 14 June 1945 from Schleswig to Eggebeck. The other two are probably the former D-AGAC and D-AKUA. Two Ju 52-3m's fitted with floats went to the British Marine Aircraft Experimental Station at Felixtowe. In January 1943 two Ju 52s fell into British hands in the Near East. These were probably machines belonging to 'Gruppe Junck' in Iraq. They subsequently flew with the British markings HK919 and HK920. HK919 was works number 5005 and was later fitted with Pratt & Whitney Wasp engines.

The history of Ju 52-3m, works number 5489, which landed at Hamburg-Fuhlsbüttel on 28 December 1984, at 1330 hours, and will – one hopes – be restored, was an adventurous one. Whether or not it will ever be capable of flying will depend on whether the many corroded parts can be renewed. This machine has been bought by Deutsche Lufthansa for this specific purpose, and it is hoped that the LH department HAM WD 4 will be able to carry out this difficult task. It was the original Lufthansa machine D-AQUI, a g2e fitted with floats, which remained at Oslo-Fornebu in May 1943. It was overhauled and subsequently flown as LN-DAH 'Falken' with th Norwegian air transport company Det Norske Luchtfahrtselskab. In 1947 it was fitted with parts from other machines and flown until 1956 as Ju 52-3mg8e LN-KAF. In 1957 it was sold, complete with 20,000 kg of spare parts, to Ecuador, where it continued in service until 1963. It was then deposited at Quito airport and left to rot until it was bought in 1970 by an American, from whom it was acquired, in turn, by the American journalist Martin Caidin. Caidin had found it in the jungle near Quito and subsequently enlisted an engine specialist from Pratt & Whitney as well as an aircraft designer from Miami to help in its rescue. After one month of hard work the team took off for Miami. Here, Caidin and a friend, Nick Silverio, took the machine entirely to pieces and put it together again. It was then bought by Lufthansa. The machine was flown by Cpt. Clark Woodard and his co-pilot John Wilson and flight mechanic Terry Ritter with much patience and resourcefulness and in several stages as far as Hamburg. It is hardly possible to say what is left of the former works number 5489.

A Casa 352 was sold to South Africa Airways from Britain. This machine has been restored to represent an early South African Airways Ju 523m, ZS-AFA. The interior has been exactly reproduced and the aircraft has been fitted with three Pratt and Whitney engines. On 1 November 1986 it received a full certificate of airworthiness and now regularly flies with fare paying passengers. It is without doubt the finest example of a passenger version of a Ju 52 flying. A further Casa 352 is approaching airworthiness in the UK; owned by Keith May, who already has one Casa 352 under his wing, it is hoped to have it available for film work in 1987.

It is impossible to say how many Ju 52s were built. The camouflage work during the build-up phase of the Luftwaffe makes it impossible to ascertain with certainty how many Ju 52s were built before 1939. In September 1939 the Luftwaffe had 547 Ju 52s. During the second World War 2804 were built, of these 326 at the Amiot works in France. After the occupation of the works a further 415 Ju 52-3mg10e's were built as AACIs. CASA in Spain produced 170 machines. This makes a total of 3922. British and American sources, on the other hand, repeatedly speak of 4845 Ju 52s. It is unlikely that this contradiction will ever be resolved. Whatever the case, the Ju 52 has a firm place in the world history of aviation although it never reached the output figures of the American Douglas DC-3 and its successors. Those who ever flew a Ju 52 and all those who ever flew in one will never forget them.

Ju 52-3mg4e A-701 of the Swiss air force after completion of its service, with civil registration markings HB-HOS. In the background a Bücker Jungmann Bü 131.

Ju-3mg4e A-702 with German markings for the film *Agenten sterben einsam* (Agents die lonely).

Ju 52-3mg4e A-703 with in original paint scheme.

Top: **The same aircraft some years later.**

Middle: **Ju 52-3mg3e, works number 5715, subsequently Royal Air Force VM985, and then PH-UBA** *Opa.*
Right: **Ju 52-3mg6e, works number 3428, subsequently Royal Air Force VM927, which became PH-UBB** *Ome Keesje.*

Ju 52-3mg10e, works number 05210078, subsequently Royal Air Force VN743, became PH-UBC *Oma*.

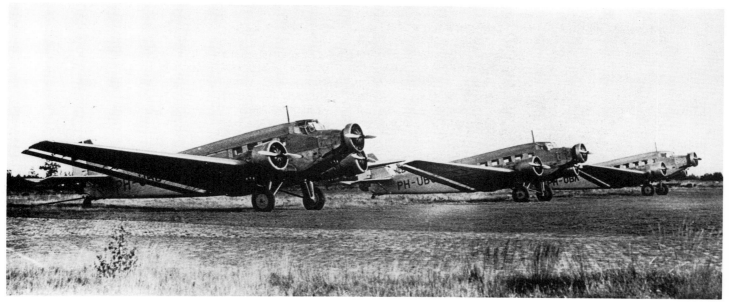

The three Ju 52-3m of the Dutch Rijksluchtvaartschool.

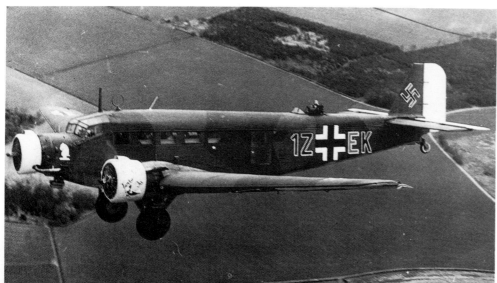

CASA 352L, lovingly restored in England, with the markings of KG zbV1.

Ju 52-3mg10e, works number 501441, subsequently Royal Air Force VM923, subsequently BEA G-AHOC.

This Ju 52-3mg10e went to Britain in 1945 as VN729 and became BEA G-AHOF.

Ju 52-3m and Siebel Si 204D after the war in Czechoslovakia.

A Ju 352 also continued to fly in Czechoslovakia for a number of years.

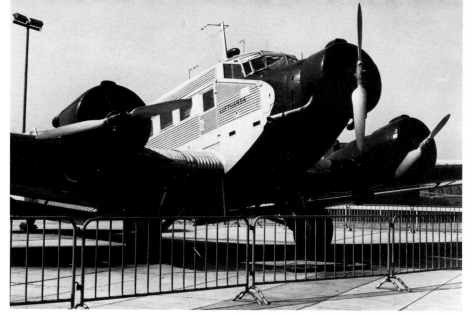

CASA 352L with German registration markings D-CIAS at Frankfurt airport.

On 28 December 1984 *Iron Annie*, parts of which were at one time works number 5489, landed at Hamburg-Fuhlsbüttel. Lufthansa, who bought the machine, hopes to introduce it to the public fully restored and, if possible, able to fly.

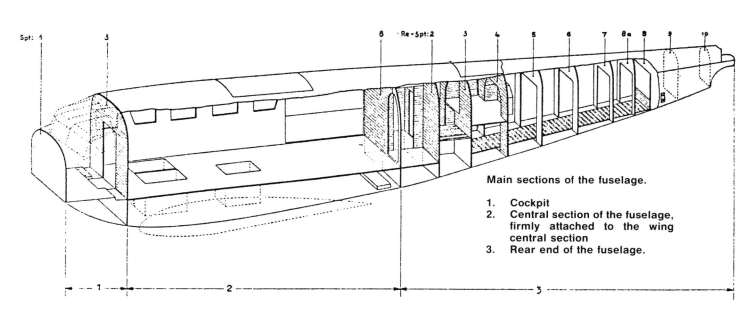

Main sections of the fuselage.

1. Cockpit
2. Central section of the fuselage, firmly attached to the wing central section
3. Rear end of the fuselage.

APPENDIX

Junkers Ju 52/1m

Ju 52be	Cargo plane with BMW VIIaU, works no. 4001, D-1974, later D-UZYP; maiden flight 13.10.1930; other versions ce, ca, ba, da, de fitted with Daimler-Benz DB 600
Ju 52bi	Works no. 4002, cargo plane with Armstrong-Siddeley Leopard, D-2133, later D-USUS, also as Ju 52ci, di, with BMW 132K.
Ju 52ce	Works no. 4003 with BMW VIIaU, D-USON, Works no. 4004, cargo plane with BMW vIIaU Cargo plane D-2317, later experiments with torpedoes as SE-ADM, subsequently towing target aircraft D-UBES
Ju 52cai	Initially cargo, later towing target aircraft with BMW IXU, works no. 4005, D-2356, burnt out May 1933 after an accident
Ju 52cao	Cargo plane with Rolls Royce Buzzard, works no. 4006, CF-ARM
Ju 52ce	Works no. 4007, D-UHYF target towing aircraft. Works no. 4008-4012 modified to Ju 52-3m.

Junkers Ju 52/3m

Ju 52m-3mbe	Works nos. 4008 and 4009, Pratt & Whitney Hornet supplied to Lloyd Aereo Boliviano as passenger aircraft, and used there as military transports in the Gran Chaco War; Works nos. 4010, 4011 and 4012 supplied as floatplanes to the Columbian Air Force, military registration nos. 621, 622, 623.
Ju 52-3mba	Passenger aircraft with 1 x Hispano-Suiza 12 Mb and 2 x Nb. Works no. 4016, CV-FAI.
Ju 52-3mce	Works no. 4013, D-2201, the first of the Ju 52s to be built as a 3-engine aircraft with Pratt & Whitney Hornet; similar

	works nos. 4014, OH-ALK, 4015, D-2202, 4017, SE-ADR, and works no. 4019, D-2468.
Ju 52-3mfe	Transport aircraft, 1933 with 3 BMW Hornet from works no. 4020; improved version with landing gear cladding and wing engines with NACA cowls.
Ju 52-3mfle	D-3012 training aircraft for DVS 1934
Ju 52-3mge	Passenger aircraft with 3 BMW Hornet later BMW 132A/E. Used by Lufthansa and abroad for passenger transport. Training of Reichswehr pilots on the Reichsbahn route Berlin-Königsberg
Ju 52-3mgle and g2e	Passenger aircraft for Lufthansa with BMW 132A/E, BMW 132A-3
Ju 52-3mgeX	Passenger aircraft, as g2e, with special equipment.
Ju 52-3m1	Passenger aircraft for Sweden with Pratt & Whitney Hornet S1eG
Ju 52-3mg	Passenger aircraft for British Airways, with Pratt & Whitney Wasp S3HI-G, and Argentina.
Ju 52-3mg	Passenger aircraft for Italy with Piaggio PXR engines
Ju 52-3mg	Passenger aircraft for Poland with Bristol Pegasus VI
Ju 52-3mho	Passenger aircraft with Jumo 205C, only works no. 4045 D-AJYR, and works no. 4055, D-AQAR for Lufthansa.
Ju 52-3mreo	Passenger aircraft with BMW 132Da/Dc for Lufthansa.
Ju 52-3mSa3	Passenger and training aircraft with BMW 132A-3 for training of Reichswehr pilots
Ju 52-3mte	Passenger aircraft with BMW 132G/L. Fastest and most highly developed of all civil versions.
Ju 52-3m12	Passenger aircraft with BMW 132L, supplied to Finland
Ju 52-3mZ/Z1	Passenger aircraft for Lufthansa with BMW 132Z-3 and improved cabin fittings
Ju 52-3mg3e	Auxiliary bomber for Luftwaffe with BMW 132A: after 1938 refitted as transport aircraft g4e

Ju 52-3mg4e	Transport aircraft with BMW 132A. Reinforced floor. Large loading hatches on the right-hand side of the fuselage and cabin roof. Reinforced landing gear. Prototype built at Weserflug, Lemwerder. Some machines were supplied to Lufthansa, three to Switzerland; these are still flying today.
Ju 52-3mg5e	Transport aircraft with BMW 132T. Landing gear interchangeable for floats of different sizes. Some fitted with 'towing gear 6000' for transport gliders. Additional armament. Serial construction from 1941
Ju 52-3mg6e	Transport aircraft, similar to g5e, but only with landing gear or landing skis.
Ju 52-3mg7e	Land and sea transport aircraft with BMW 132T. Extended loading hatch, side windows reduced. Siemens K4ü navigational instruments
Ju 52-3mg8e	Transport aircraft similar to g6e, but with additional K4ü instrumentation
Ju 52-3mg9e	Transport aircraft similar to g6e, but BMW 132Z and other equipment
Ju 52-3mg10e	Land and Sea Transport aircraft. BMW 132T. Series construction by Weserflug and Amiot.
Ju 52-3mgl2e	Similar to g10e, but only small series with BMW 132L.
Ju 52-3mgl4e	Similar to g8e, but improved reinforcement.
Ju 52-3mMS	Conversion of a number of Ju 52-3mg4e-g6e to mine-detection aircraft
Ju 52-3m	Built in Spain and France after 1945.

Technical data Junkers Ju 52be
(according to Junkers prospectus V.61/7.31)

Dimensions
Length	18.50m
Wingspan	29.50m
Wing	110m²

Weights
Dry weight (total)	3890kg

Flying weight	normal 6600 kg	approved by DVL 7000 kg
Total cargo	normal 2710 kg	3110 kg
Crew (2)	160 kg	
Crew baggage	25 kg	
Fuel for 1000 km passenger flight	680 kg	700 kg
Payload	1845 kg	2225 kg

Performance
Cargo compartment total, in m³	23.125
Wing loading in kg/m²	63.3
Power loading in kg/hp	9.65
Engine performance in hp	685
Maximum speed, low altitude	194 km/h
Cruising speed, low altitude	160 km/h
Landing speed	77-80 km/h
Rate of climb, 1000 m	9.8 minutes
Rate of climb, 2000 m	22.4 minutes
Rate of climb, 3000 m	42.9 minutes
Operating ceiling	2800 m
Absolute ceiling	4200 m
Take-off distance	255 m
Landing distance	155 m
Share of payload in flying weight in %, 1000 km range	32%

Technical description Ju 52-3mge

Airframe:

Wing assembly, arrangement: low-wing cantilever monoplane; wings tapering in chord and thickness towards the tips; wings designed on Junkers 'high lift' principle; full-span ailerons in two sections, with inboard section action as flap/airbrake.

Fuselage, arrangement: in front central engine; behind that enclosed cockpit with two seats side-by-side, heating and ventilation; if equipped with a small radio station tip-up seat for radio operator in the flight deck; where fitted with large radio transmitter, direction finder etc. special compartment behind cockpit; passenger cabin consisting of smokers' section with 4, and non-smokers' section with 13, adjustable leather seats; noise-insulated cabin walls, adjustable warm-air heating and ventilation; behind the cabin lavatory, luggage area; below the cabin in the wing centre-section four small luggage holds.

Tail unit and rudder arrangement: tail surface construction as for wing; trimmable rudder with mass balance; tail plane attached and braced to top of fuselage; separate elevators with external trim; rudder supported on ball-bearings.

Materials and general design: all-metal construction; basic material Duralumin, welded parts from chrome molybdenum steel, also use of Silumin, Elektron and more rarely Hydronalium; cladding on wings and fuselage from corrugated metal sheeting.

Design of primary structure: three main and one subsidiary frames, whose upper and lower flanges consist of hollow tubing; several cross members; cladding from corrugated metal sheeting; wing centre-section firmly attached to fuselage. Wing outer-sections attached by eight ball joints each.

Design of the fuselage: rectangular cross-section, rounded corners; four longitudinal spars, ribs, anchoring wire, stressed skin.

Design of the tail plane: longitudinal hollow tube spars and main spar, ribs, and cladding from corrugated metal sheeting.

Landing gear: in two sections; each half consisting of a forked main leg with oil or air operated shock-absorber and support strut. Main wheel with internally acting compressed air brake; detachable streamlined fairing; castoring tail wheel, air or oil shock-absorber and hydraulic brake.

Floats: two twin-keel, single-stage floats attached to braced hollow tube structure.

Crew: 2 or 3 man crew, 17 passengers.

Engines:

Arrangement and attachment: Fore-end of fuselage and leading edge of outer wings; engine supported on triangulated tubular mountings attached by ball joints to wings and fuselage; central engine with Townend ring, wing engines with rings similar to NACA cowls.

Engines: 3 BMW 132A (nine-cylinder radial engine)

Engine performance: 3 x 660 hp

Propellers: metal; 2 blades; adjustable pitch

Cooling: air

Fuel storage: 4 tanks in each of the outer wings; 1 gravity tank in the fuselage

Fuel capacity: 1370 litres

Fuel supply: 3 Jumo pumps and one hand pump

Lubricant storage: one tank each (approx. 68 ltr.) behind fireproof bulkhead.

Dimensions, weights, performance and requirements:

	Landplane (both)		Floatplane
Wingspan		29.25 m	
Length	18.90 m		19.20 m
Height	6.10 m		7.30 m
Aspect ratio		1:7.82	
Dihedral angle		7° 2'	
Wing		110.5 m²	
Empty weight	5900 kg		6530 kg
Total cargo	4100 kg		3470 kg
Flying weight	10000 kg		10000 kg
Wing loading		90.5 kg/m²	
Power loading		5.06 kg/hp	
Power/wing area loading		17.9 hp/m²	
Maximum speed (at 915 m)	300 km/h		290 km/h
Maximum permissible cruising speed (at 2500 m)	283 km/h		270 km/h
Economical cruising speed (at 2500 m)	270 km/h		260 km/h
Landing speed		104 km/h	
Range (ec. cruising speed)	1500 km		1200 km
Rate of climb to 1000 m	4.1 min		4.3 min
Rate of climb to 3000 m	14.5 min		15.5 min
Ceiling	6600 m		6400 m
Fuel consumption, most economical cruising speed	113 l/100 km		117 l/100 km

Comparison of Ju 52 versions: from prototype to production aircraft

Manufacturer		Junkers	Junkers	Junkers	Junkers	Junkers	Junkers
Model		G24a	Ju 52/1m	Ju 52/3mce[1]	Ju 52/3mce[2]	Ju 52/3mg[3]	Ju 52/3m built 1938
Engine(s)		Junkers L 2a 3 x 230 = 690 PS	BMW VII all 685 PS	BMW Hornet A 2 3 x 525 = 1575 PS	BMW Hornet A 2 3 x 525 = 1575 PS	Pratt u. Whitney Wasp S 3 H 1-G 3 x 558 = 1674 PS[4]	Pratt u. Whitney Hornet S 1 E-G 3 x 715 = 2145 PS[7]
Crew (+ passengers)		2 + 9	2	2	2 + 17	2 + 17	2 + 17
Length	m	15.23	18.50	18.50	18.90	18.90	18.90
Height	m	5.50	4.65	4.65	6.10	6.10	6.10
Wingspan	m	28.05	29.50	29.25	29.25	29.25	29.25
Wing area	m²	99.00	110.00	110.50	110.50	110.50	110.50
Aspect ratio		8	7.91	7.74	7.74	7.74	7.74
Dry weight		3 700	4 015	5 360	5 970	6 370	6 600
Fuel	kg	720	700	1 165	1 115	1 065	1 080
Lubricant	kg	95	105	150	150	185	185
Crew	kg	180	180	180	180	180	180
Payload	kg	805	2 000	2 145	1 795	2 200	2 455
Total cargo	kg	1 800	2 985	3 640	3 240	3 630	3 900
Flying weight	kg	5 500	7 000	9 000	9 210	10 000	10 500
Wing loading	kg/m²	55.50	63.60	81.44	83.35	90.50	95.02
Power loading	kg/hp	7.97	10.20	5.71	5.85	5.98	4.89
Specific payload	kg/hp	1.17	2.92	2.36	1.14	1.31	0.81
Power/wing area loading	hp/m²	6.97	6.22	14.25	14.25	15.15	19.41
Maximum speed	km/h	175	195	235	271	284	315
at altitude	m	0	0	0	900	1 525	2 100
Cruising speed	km/h	155	160	185	222	250	295
at altitude	m	0	0	0	900	3 600	3 200
Rate of climb	m/s			3.20	3.90	4.20	6.00
Operating ceiling	m	4 000	3 800	4 800	5 200	5 800[5]	6 500[8]
Range	km	850	1 000	925	950	1 060[8]	850[9]
Take-off distance	m	200	180	290	340	300	320
Landing distance	m	200	175	240	245	330	350
Landing speed	km/h	100	80	92	99	104	107
Cargo in % of flying weight		33.00	42.70	40.00	35.00	36.00	37.00
Payload in % of flying weight		14.60	30.40	24	19	22	23
Year of construction		1926	1930	1931	1932	1937	1938

[1] Prototype
[2] First production type for trials to Lufthansa, 1932 winner of Alpine tour competition.
[3] Hamilton variable pitch, constant speed propeller.
[4] Fuel consumption 234 kg/h, cruising at 3600 m; oil consumption 7.5% of fuel consumption.
[5] Maximum height in case of one engine failing at 10000 kg flying weight, 3100 m
[6] At 3600 m including horizontal and ascending flight.
[7] Hamilton variable pitch, constant speed propeller.
[8] 3500 m in case of one engine failing and full flying weight.
[9] The fuel installation had a capacity of 2400 l = 1760 kg, which meant a range of 1500 km with a payload of 1740 kg.

Technical data

	Ju 252	Ju 352
Crew	4	4
Wingspan m	34.09	34.21
Length m	25.10	24.60
Height m	5.75	5.75
Wing area m²	122.6	128.2
Empty weight kg	13100	12500
Payload kg	5450	4300
Take-off weight kg	22000	19500
Engines	Jumo 211F	Bramo 323 R-2
Take-off power hp	3 x 1350	3 x 1200
Cruising power at 5500 m hp	3 x 920	3 x 660
Maximum speed km/h	438	370
Fighting speed (30 min) km/h	417	330
Cruising speed km/h	335	240
Landing speed km/h	120	120
Operating ceiling m	6300	6000
Range km, max load	3980	3025
Range, 2000 kg load, km	6600	–
Armament	1xMG131 2xMG15	1xMG151/20
Paint, upper side	dark green 71	dark green 71 black/green 70
Paint, under side	light blue 65	light blue 65

Junkers Ju 52s in international air transport

Argentina

LV-AAB		Aeroposta Argentina *Patagonia*
LV-AAJ		Aeroposta Argentina *Ibate*
LV-BAB		Aeroposta Argentina *Tierra del Fuego*
LV-CAB		Aeroposta Argentina

Australia (New Guinea)

VH-BUU	7256	Gibbes Sepik Airways Ex SE-BUE, OH-LAM	D-AVIU
VH-BUV	7493	Gibbes Sepik Airways Ex SE-BUD & OH-LAO	VH-GSS
VH–BUW	641375	Gibbes Sepik Airways Ex SE-AYB & OY-DFU	VH-GSW

Belgium

OO-AGU	5510	Sabena
OO-AGV	5514	Sabena
OO-AGW	5672	Sabena
OO-AUA	5815	Sabena
OO-AUB	5827	Sabena
OO-AUF	5852	Sabena
OO-AUG	6063*	Sabena
OO-AUK	6410	Sabena
OO-CAP	5518	Sabena Ex G-AERX → SE–AES

Bolivia

Juan del Valle	4008	Lloyd Aereo Boliviano
Huanuni	4009	Lloyd Aereo Boliviano
Chorolque	4018	Lloyd Aereo Boliviano
Bolivar	4061	Lloyd Aereo Boliviano

Brazil

PP-CAT	4024	Syndicato Condor *Anhangá*	
PP-CAV	4038	Syndicato Condor *Caicara*	
PP-CAX	4043	Syndicato Condor *Gurupira*	Ex D-ABIS
PP-CAY	4042	Syndicato Condor *Marimbá*	Ex D-3136
PP-CAZ	5261	Syndicato Condor *Maipo*	Ex D-AGST
PP-CBA	5283	Syndicato Condor *Aconcagua* → D-AENF	
PP-CBB	4078	Syndicato Condor *Tupan*	
PP-CBC	5453	Syndicato Condor *Guaracy*	
PP-CBD	5478	Syndicato Condor *Jacy*	Ex D-AJAO
PP-CBE	5100	Syndicato Condor *Larussu*	
PP-CBF	4079	Syndicato Condor *Arocy or Aeluss*	Ex D-APOR
PP-CBG	4075	Syndicato Condor *Pagé*	Ex D-APEF
PP-CBH	5109	Syndicato Condor	Ex HC-SND → D-AMAQ
PP-CBL	5656	Syndicato Condor	Ex D-AMYE
PP-CBP	6800	Syndicato Condor	Ex D-AHGB
PP-CBR	5053	Syndicato Condor	Ex D-AQUQ
PP-SPD	5459	VASP *Cidade do S.Paulo*	
PP-SPE	5465	VASP *Cidade do Rio de Janeiro*	
PP-SPF	5689	VASP *Cidade de Santos*	
PP-VAL	4058	Varig	Ex ZS-AFA
	4025	Syndicato Condor	Ex-D-AHIH

Czechoslovakia

OK-PCC	ČSA
OK-PDC	ČSA
OK-TOI	ČSA
OK-ZDO	ČSA

Denmark

OY-DAL	5610	DDL *Selandia*	
OY-DFU	641375	DDL *Uffe Vikingf*; SAS SE-AYB, VH-BUW VH-GSW	
OY-DFY		DDL *Trym Viking*	

Germany

D-2201	4013	DLH *Boelcke*	later D-ADOM
D-2202	4015	DLH *Richthofen*	later D-ADYL
D-2468	4019	DLH	later D-AFIR
D-2490	4020	DLH *Gustav Doerr*	later D-AFYS
D-2526	4023	DLH *Zephir*	later D-AGAV
D-2527	4022	DLH *Manfred von Richthofen*	later D-AGUK
D-2588	4025	DLH *Rudolf Kleine*	later D-AHIH
D-2600	4021	DLH *Immelmann*	later D-AHUT
D-2624	4026	DLH *Rudolf Berthold*	later D-AJAN
D-2640	4027	DLH	later D-AZEV
D-2649	4028	DLH *Hermann Göring*	later D-AJUX
D-2650	4029	DLH *Fritz Rumey*	later D-AKEP
D-2725	4030	DLH *Paul Bäumer*	later D-AKOK
D-3049	4035	DLH *Heinrich Gontermann*	later D-ALAS
D-3050	4036	DLH *Kurt Wintgens*	later D-ALUN
D-3051	4037	DLH *Kurt Wüsthoff*	later D-AMAM
D-3123	4039	DLH *Gustav Leffers*	later D-ANAL
D-3127	4040	DLH *Otto Parschau*	later D-APAR
D-3131	4041	DLH *Werner Voss*	later D-ARAM
D-3136	4042	DLH *Paul Billik*	later D-ASEN
D-AAYF		DLH	
D-ABAL		DLH	
D-ABAN	4044	DLH *Emil Thuy*	
D-ABAQ		DLH *Manfred von Richthofen*	
D-ABAT		DLH	
D-ABED	6046	DLH *Viktor Neübrand*	
D-ABES	5026	DLH *Hermann Thomsen*; → *Fritz Röth*	
D-ABEW	6432	DLH *Rudolf von Thüna*	
D-ABFA	6385	DLH *Otto Parschau*	
D-ABIK	4069	DLH *Manfred von Richthofen*	
D-ABIS	4043	DLH Syndicato Condor PP-CAX	
D-ABIZ	4068	DLH *Erich Albrecht*	
D-ABON	5237	DLH	
D-ABUR	5777	DLH *Charles Haar*	
D-ABVF	5954	DLH *Franz Wagner*	
D-ABYF		DLH *Hans Kirschstein*	
D-ACBE	6550	DLH *Emil Schäfer*	
D-ACBO	4059	DLH *v. Neubrandt*	Ex ZS-AFD
D-ACEP	6386	DLH *A. v. Tutschek*	
D-ADAL	4046	DLH *Karl Allmenröder*; Deruluft *Flamingo*	
D-ADBO	6387	DLH *Olivier von Beaulieu-Marconnay*	
D-ADBW	6650	DLH *Emil Thuy*	
D-ADED		DLH	
D-ADEF	4070	DLH *Adolf Schirmer*	
D-ADEK	5278	DLH *Anton Schulz*	
D-ADER	5120	DLH *Hans Wende*; Syndicato Condor PP-CBE	
D-ADHF	6066	DLH *Walter Höhndorf*	
D-ADIH		DLH	
D-ADIP	5102	DLH	
D-ADIT		DLH	
D-ADOM	4013	DLH *Boelcke*	Ex D-2201
D-ADQU	640605	DLH *Karl Noack*	
D-ADQV	640608	DLH *Hermann Stache*	
D-ADQW	640610	DLH *Harry Rother*	
D-ADYL	4015	DLH *Richthofen*	Ex D-2202
D-AEAO	6670	DLH *R Fritsche*	
D-AEHE		DLH	
D-AENF	5283	DLH *Aconcagua*; Syndicato Condor PP-CBA	
D-AFAM		DLH *Max von Müller*	
D-AFCD	5938	DLH *Erich Albrecht*	
D-AFEH		DLH	
D-AFEP		DLH	
D-AFER	4047	DLH *Franz Büchner*	later D-AFES
D-AFES	4047	DLH *Franz Büchner*	Ex D-AFER
D-AFFQ	6057	DLH *G. Falke*	
D-AFIR	4019	DLH	Ex D-2468
D-AFOP	5800	DLH *Karl Hochmuth*	
D-AFOR		DLH	
D-AFYS	4020	DLH *Gustav Doerr*	Ex D-2490
D-AGAK	5685	DLH *Ulrich Neckel*	
D-AGAL		DLH	
D-AGAV	4023	DLH *Zephir*; later *Emil Schäfer*	Ex D-2526
D-AGBI	6659	DLH *M. von Mulzer*	
D-AGDA	4080	DLH *Wedigo v. Froreich*	
D-AGEI	5472	DLH *Karl Allmenröder*	
D-AGES	5104	DLH *Otto Kissenberth*	Eurasia XVII
D-AGFD	4060	DLH *Otto Parschau*; to Iberia EC-AAI	Ex ZS-AFC
D-AGIQ	5272	DLH *Martin Zander*	later D-ASIQ
D-AGIS	4048	DLH *Wilhelm Schmidt & M. v. Müller*; Deruluft *Kormoran*	
D-AGOB	6452	DLH *H. Handke*	
D-AGOO	5555	DLH *Fritz Simon*	
D-AGST	5261	DLH *Maipo*; Syndicato Condor PP-CAZ	
D-AGTC	6030	DLH *Wilhelm Cuno*	

D-AGUK	4022	DLH *Manfred von Richthofen;*		
		Kurt Wolff	Ex D-2527	
D-AGYS		DLH		
D-AHAL	5034	DLH *Otto Bernert*		
D-AHEK		DLH		
D-AHEP	5195	DLH		
D-AHFN	6047	DLH *H. Krickelsdor*		
D-AHGA	6775	DLH *Paul Billik*		
D-AHGB	6800	DLH *Rudolf Kleine;*		
		Syndicato Condor PP-CBP		
D-AHIH	4025	DLH *Rudolf Kleine*	Ex D-2588	
D-AHIT	4053	DLH *Immelmann*	Ex D-AXAN	
			H.J. Buddecke	
D-AHLF		DLH		
D-AHMS	6042	DLH *Martin Zander*		
D-AHUL		DLH		
D-AHUR		DLH		
D-AHUS	4049	DLH *Heinrich Kroll;* Deruluft *Milan*		
D-AHUT	4021	DLH *Immelmann;*	Ex D-2600	
		H. J. Buddecke		
D-AHUX		DLH		
D-AHYN		DLH		
D-AIAG	7244	DLH *O. Bielenstein*		
D-AIAH	7268	DLH *K. Hochmuth*		
D-AIAO		DLH		
D-AITY		DLH		
D-AJAN	4026	DLH *Rudolf Berthold*	Ex D-2624	
D-AJAO	5478	DLH *Robert Weichard;*		
		Syndicato Condor PP-CBD		
D-AJAT		DLH		
D-AJIM	4050	DLH *Hermann Göring*		
D-AJUP	5068	DLH		
D-AJUX	4028	DLH *Ulrich Neckel*	Ex D-2649	
D-AJYR	4045	DLH *Emil Schaefer*		
D-AKEP	4029	DLH *Fritz Rumey*	Ex D-2650	
D-AKEQ	5590	DLH *Gust. Rubritiüs*		
D-AKIQ		DLH		
D-AKIY	5429	DLH *William Langanke;* DNL LN-DAF		
D-AKOK	4030	DLH *Paul Bäumer*	Ex D-2725	
D-AKOX		DLH		
D-AKUA		DLH		
D-AKUO	5484	DLH *Paul Billik*		
D-AKUT		DLH		
D-AKYS	5098	DLH *Emil Thuy;*	Iberia EC-AAH	
D-ALAM	5740	DLH *Wilhelm Langanke*		
D-ALAN	5010	DLH *Eduard Dostler*		
D-ALAP		DLH		
D-ALAS	4035	DLH *Heinrich Gontermann*	Ex D-3049	
D-ALEF	5011	DLH		
D-ALOS		DLH		
D-ALUE	5502	DLH *Joachim von Schröder*		
D-ALUG		DLH		
D-ALUN	4036	DLH *Kurt Wintgens*	Ex D-3050	
D-ALUS		DLH		
D-ALYL	5180	DLH *Hans Loeb;* then *Linke-Crawford*		
		became „XI. Olympiade 1936"		
D-AMAK	5294	DLH *Volkmar von Arnim*		
D-AMAM	4037	DLH *Kurt Wüsthoff*	Ex D-3051	
D-AMAQ	5109	DLH *Max von Mulzer;* HC-SND PP-CBH		
D-AMEI	5734	DLH *F. v. Roeth*		
D-AMFR	5933	DLH *Ludwig Hautzmeyer*		
D-AMIP	4072	DLH *Fritz Erb*		
D-AMIT	5060	DLH *O. v. Beaulieu-Marconnay*		
D-AMON		DLH		
D-AMYE	5656	DLH *Los Andes;*		
		Syndicato Condor PP-CBL		
D-AMYR		DLH		
D-AMYY		DLH *Wilhelm Siegert*		
D-ANAL	4039	DLH *Gustav Leffers*	Ex D-3123	
D-ANAO		DLH *Joachim von Schröder*		
D-ANAZ	5128	DLH *Willi Charlett*		
D-ANCY		DLH		
D-ANEH		DLH		
D-ANEN	5072	DLH *Fritz Puetter*		
D-ANJH	5747	DLH *Hans Loeb*		
D-ANOL	5014	DLH *Albert Dossenbach*		
D-ANOP	4077	DLH *Fr. Simon;*	DNL LN-DAE	
D-ANOY	5663	DLH *Rudolf von Thüna*		
D-ANUT		DLH		
D-ANXG	5979	DLH *Hans Kirschstein*		
D-ANYF	4071	DLH *Erich Pust*		
D-ANYK	5329	DLH *Wilhelm Schmidt*		
D-AONU		DLH		
D-APAA		DLH *Otto Kissenbert*		
D-APAJ	7029	DLH *E. Pust*		
D-APAR	4040	DLH *Otto Parschau*	Ex D-3127	
D-APDF		DLH		
D-APEF	4075	DLH *Karl Wessel*		
		Syndicato Condor PP-CBG		
D-APEH	5233	DLH		
D-APGU	6734	DLH *Bruno Rodschinka*		
D-APIR		DLH		
D-APOK	5074	DLH *Max von Müller*		
D-APOO		DLH		
D-APOR	4079	DLH *Olaf Bieberstein;*		
		Syndicato Condor PP-CBF		
D-APUP	5682	DLH *Marschall von Bieberstein*		
D-APXD	6149	DLH *Robert Untucht*		

Reg.	No.	Operator / Name	Notes
D-APYX	5055	DLH	
D-APZX	6750	DLH *Raoul Stoisvljevic*	VM 908 G-AHBP
D-AQAM		DLH Deutsche Reichsbahngesellschaft	
D-AQAR	4055	DLH *W. Höhndorf*	
D-AQEX		DLH *Heinrich Kroll*	
D-AQIT		DLH *Major Dincklage*	
D-AQUI	5489	DLH	DNL LN-DAH
D-AQUQ	5053	DLH *Adolf v. Tutschek;* Syndicato Condor PP-CBR	
D-AQUT		DLH	
D-ARAD	6171	DLH *Volkmar von Arnim*	
D-ARAM	4041	DLH *Werner Voss*	Ex D-3131
D-ARCK	6779	DLH *Van Vloten*	
D-ARDS	5919	DLH *Robert Weichard*	
D-AREB	6442	DLH *Charles Haar*	
D-AREN		DLH	Deruluft
D-ARES		DLH	
D-ARET		DLH *K. Schumann*	
D-ARIW	6180	DLH *Joachim Blankenburg*	
D-ARUW		DLH	
D-ARVU	6790	DLH *Hans Wende*	
D-ARYS	5043	DLH *Hans Kirschstein*	
D-ASDI	7077	DLH *R. Kleine*	
D-ASEE		DLH	
D-ASEN	4042	DLH *Paul Billik* Ex D-3136 Syndicato Condor PP-CAY	
D-ASEV		DLH	
D-ASFD	6014	DLH *Heinrich Mathy*	
D-ASHY	7089	DLH *G. Doerr*	
D-ASIH	5078	DLH *Rudolf Windisch*	
D-ASIQ	5272	DLH *M. Zander*	Ex D-AGIQ
D-ASIS	4074	DLH *Wilhelm Cuno*	
D-ASLG	6369	DLH *Alfred Viereck*	
D-ASUI		DLH *Hans Berr*	
D-ASYF		DLH	
D-ATAK	5169	DLH *Marschall v. Bieberstein*	
D-ATAO	5748	DLH *Alfred Bauer*	
D-ATAQ		DLH	
D-ATAT		DLH	
D-ATAV		DLH *Alfred Bauer*	
D-ATAW	7160	DLH *Lothar von Richthofen*	
D-ATDB	5940	DLH *Walter Bayer*	
D-ATEA	5727	DLH *Philipp von Blaschke*	
D-ATOL		DLH Deutsche Reichsbahngesellschaft	
D-ATON	4054	DLH *Erwin Böhme*	
D-ATUF		DLH *Graf Schlieffen*	
D-ATVO		DLH	
D-ATYZ	5797	*Hans Hackmack*	
D-AUAV		DLH	
D-AUAX		DLH	
D-AUJA	5851	DLH	Iberia EC-AAF
D-AUJG	5942	DLH *Hans Wende*	
D-AUKE	5858	DLH	
D-AUSS		DLH *Josef Langheld*	
D-AUXZ	7172	DLH *B. Marconnay*	
D-AVAJ	6370	DLH *Olaf Bielenstein*	
D-AVAN		Deutsche Reichsbahngesellschaft	
D-AVAU		DLH	
D-AVES		DLH Deutsche Reichsbahngesellschaft	
D-AVFB		DLH	
D-AVIR	5019	DLH Deutsche Reichsbahngesellschaft	
D-AVIU	7256	DLH *Th. Schöpwinkel;* Aero O/Y OH-LAM	
D-AVUL	4073	DLH *Bruno Rodschinka;* Iberia EC-AAJ	
D-AVUP	5267	DLH *Kurt Steidel*	
D-AVYO		DLH	
D-AWAS	6561	DLH *Joachim Blankenburg*	
D-AXAF		DLH	
D-AXAN	4053	DLH *H. J. Buddecke;* D-AHIT *Immelmann*	
D-AXAT	5693	DLH *Rudolf Windisch*	
D-AXES	4052	DLH *Hans Berr;* Deruluft *Kondor*	
D-AXFH	6372	DLH *H. E. Lochner*	
D-AXOP	5189	DLH	
D-AXOS	5023	DLH *Oswald Boelcke*	
D-AXUT	5022	DLH *Lothar von Richthofen;* Iberia EC-AAG	
D-AYAZ		DLH	
D-AYGX	7208	DLH *Johannes Höroldt*	
D-AYHO	5860	DLH *Peter Strasser*	
D-AYKU		DLH	
D-AZAN	5021	DLH *J. v. Schröder*	
D-AZAZ		DLH	
D-AZEV	4027	DLH	Ex D-2640
D-AZIR	1301*	DLH *Fritz Erb*	
D-AZIS	5020	DLH *von Bülow; Horst Wessel*	

Equador

Reg.	No.	Operator / Name
HC-SND	5109	Sociedad Ecuatoriana de Transportes Aereos SA Ex D-AMAQ → PP-CBH

Estonia

Reg.	Operator
ES-AUL	AGO

Finland

Reg.	No.	Operator / Name	Notes
OH-ALK	4014	Aero O/Y *Sampo*	later OH-LAK
OH-ALL	5494	Aero O/Y *Kaleva*	
OH-LAM	7256	Aero O/Y *Karjala*	SE-BUE VH-BUU Ex D-AVIU
OH-LAO	7493	Aero O/Y *Waasa*	SE-BUD, VH-BUV VH-GSS

OH-LAP	7490	Aero O/Y	*Petsamo*

France (In Frankreich gebaute AAC. 1)

Reg.	c/n	Operator	Notes
F-BAJA	001	Air France	
F-BAJB	002	Air France	
F-BAJC	003	Air France	
F-BAJD	004	Air France	
F-BAJE	005	Air France	
F-BAJG	006	Air France	
F-BAJH	007	Air France	
			F-BBOF
F-BAJI	008	Air France	
F-BAJJ	013	Air France	
F-BAJK	014	Air France	
F-BAJL	015	Air France	
F-BAJM	016	Air France	*Oradour*
F-BAJN	017	Air France	
F-BAJO	018	Air France	
F-BAJP	019	Air France	
F-BAJS	020	Air France	
F-BAJT	044	Air France	
F-BAJU	036	Air France	
F-BAJV	037	Air France	
F-BAJX	038	Air France	
F-BAKK	101	Air France	
F-BAKL	102	Air France	
F-BAKM	055	Air France	
F-BAKN	056	Air France	
F-BAKO	057	Air France	
F-BAKP	058	Air France	
F-BAKQ	059	Air France	
F-BAKR	060	Air France	
F-BAKS	071	Air France	
F-BAKT	072	Air France	
F-BAKU	073	Air France	Cie Gle de Transport LR-AAC *Beiteddine*
F-BAKV	074	Air France	
F-BAKX	075	Air France	
F-BAKY	076	Air France	
F-BAKZ	077	Air France	
F-BALA	078	Air France	
F-BALB	079	Air France	
F-BALC	080	Air France	
F-BALD	103	Air France	
F-BALE	090	Air France	
F-BALF	091	Air France	
F-BALG	092	Air France	
F-BALH	093	Air France	
F-BALI	094	Air France	
F-BALJ	095	Air France	
F-BALK	096	Air France	
F-BALL	097	Air France	
F-BALM	098	Air France	
F-BALN	099	Air France	
F-BALO	100	Air France	
F-BAMO	104	Air France	
F-BAMP	105	Air France	
F-BAMQ	106	Air France	
F-BAMR	107	Air France	
F-BAMS	108	Air France	
F-BAMT	109	Air France	Cie Gle de Transport L-RAMT; later LR-AAJ *Safa*
F-BAMU	110	Air France	
F-BAMV	111	Air France	
F-BAMX	112	Air France	
F-BAMY	113	Air France	Cie Gle de Transport L-RAMY; later LR-AAI *El Arz*
F-BAMZ	114	Air France	
F-BANA	115	Air France	
F-BANB	136	Air France	
F-BANC	137	Air France	
F-BANE	139	Air France	
F-BANF	140	Air France	
F-BANG	141	Air France	
F-BANH	142	Air France	
F-BANI	143	Air France	
F-BANJ	144	Air France	
F-BANK	145	Air France	
F-BANL	146	Air France	
F-BANM	147	Air France	
F-BANN	148	Air France	F-BDYK; Portugal CS-ADA
F-BANO	149	Air France	
F-BANP	150	Air France	
F-BANQ	151	Air France	
F-BANR	152	Air France	
F-BANS	153	Air France	
F-BBYG	227	Air France	
F-BBYH	228	Air France	
F-BBYI	229	Air France	

F-BBYJ	195	Air France	
F-BBYK	231	TAI	
F-BBYL	232	TAI	
F-BBYM	233	TAI	
F-BBYN	234	TAI	
F-BBYP	236	Sté Aéro-Cargo	
F-BBYT	240	Air Atlas	
F-BBZA	246	SANA *Kerguern*	
F-BBZE	250	Aigle Azur	
F-BBZF	194	SANA	
F-BBZG	196	SANA	
F-BBZH	197	SANA	
F-BBZI	202	SANA	
F-BBZJ	203	SANA	
F-BBZK	204	SANA *Kerjean*	
F-BBZL	230	Air Atlas	
F-BCHA	312	TAI	
F-BCHB	310	Sté Aéro-Cargo	
F-BCHG	324	TAI	
F-BCHJ	315	Air France; Air Atlas *Ville d'Oudjda*	
F-BCHK	316	Air Atlas *Ville de Marrakech*	
F-BCHL	317	Air Atlas *Ville de Rabat*	
F-BCHM	318	Air Atlas	
F-BCHN	319	Air Atlas	
F-BCHO	320	Air Atlas *Ville de Safi*	
F-BCHP	321	Air France; Air Atlas *Ville de Mogador*	
F-BCHQ	322	Air Atlas	
F-BCHX	381	TAI	
F-BCHY	387	TAI Aigle Azur	
F-BDYA	382	Aigle Azur	
F-BDYE	404	SANA	

Greece

SX-ACF	5984	SHCA later VM 980
SX-ACH	6004	SHCA later VM 980
SX-ACI	6025	SHCA later VM 980

Great Britain

G-AERU	5440	British Airways *Juno*	Ex SE-AER
G-AERX	5518	British Airways *Jupiter*	Ex SE-AES
			OO-CAP
G-AFAP	5881	British Airways *Jason*	
G-AHBP	6750	Railway Air Services	Ex VM 908
			D-APZX
G-AHOC	501441	British European Airways	Ex VM 923
G-AHOD	131150	British European Airways	Ex VN 740
G-AHOE		British European Airways	Ex VN 723
G-AHOF		British European Airways	Ex VN 729
G-AHOG	3317*	British European Airways	Ex VM 979
G-AHOH	641364	British European Airways	Ex VN 746
G-AHOI	641227	British European Airways	Ex VN 744
G-AHOJ	500138	British European Airways	Ex VN 756
G-AHOK	2998*	British European Airways	Ex VN 742
G-AHOL	641213	British European Airways	Ex VN 741

Italy

I-ABJZ	5492	Ala Littoria	
I-BAUS	4063	Ala Littoria	
I-BAZI		Ala Littoria	
I-BEZI	4062	Ala Littoria	
I-BIZI	4064	Ala Littoria	became AI+AO
I-BIOS	6710		became AS+PI
I-BOAN			became AI+AT
I-BERO	6803		became AS+PE

Mozambique

CR-AAJ	5962	DETA *Lourenço Marques*
CR-AAK	5967	DETA *Quelimane*
CR-AAL	5973	DETA *Nampula*

Norway

LN-DAE	4077	DNL *Havørn (Sea Eagle)*	Ex D-ANOP
LN-DAF	5429	DNL *Najaden (Naiad)*	N-KAG
LN-DAH	5489	DNL *Falken (The Falcon)*	
LN-DAI	5751	DNL *Hauken (The Hawk)*	
LN-KAD	130712	DNL *Per (Peter)*; to SAS	
LN-KAE	130704	DNL *Pål (Paul)*; to SAS	
LN-KAF	130714	DNL *Askeladden*; to SAS	
LN-KAG	5429	DNL *Veslefrikk*; to SAS	Ex LN-DAF
LN-KAI	3257	DNL *Peik*	

Austria

OE-LAK	4076	Stoisavljevic	became D-AJAT, M-CABC, EC-AAK
OE-LAL	5289		Totalbruch 16.3.1936
OE-LAM	4080	Froreich	became D-AGDA
OE-LAN	5590	Rubritius	became D-AKEQ = SG+BM
OE-LAP	5727	Blaschke	became D-ATEA
OE-LAR	5180	Linke-Crawford	became D-ALYL „XI. OLYMPIADE 1936"
OE-LAS	5933	Hautzmayer	became D-AMFR = NG+VE

Peru

OA-HHA

Poland

SP-AKX	5588	LOT	became BOAC as G-AGAE

Romania

CV-FAI	4016	LARES	became later YR-ABF

South Africa

ZS-AFA	4058	Jan van Riebeeck	became PP-VAL
ZS-AFB	4057	Lord Charles Somerset	
ZS-AFC	4060	Simon van der Stel	became EC-AAI
ZS-AFD	4059	Sir Benjamin d'Urban	
ZS-AJF		Andries Pretorius	became Earl of Caledon
ZS-AJG		Piet Retief	became Erasmus Smit
ZS-AJH	5792	Erasmus Smit	became Sir John Cradock
ZS-AJI		Major Warden	became President Burgers
ZS-AJJ		Sir George Grey	became Sir Henry Pottinger
ZS-AKY		Earl of Caledon	
ZS-ALD		Jan van Riebeeck	
ZS-ALP		Louis Botha	became Lord Charles Somerset
ZS-ALR		Paul Krüger	became Simon van der Stel
ZS-ALS		Harry Smith	became Thomas Holstead
ZS-ALUZ		Sir Peregrine Maitland	became Major Warden

Sweden

SE-ADR	4017	AB Aerotransport *Södermanland*
SE-AER	5440	AB Aerotransport *Västmanland*; to British Airways G-AERU
SE-AES	5518	AB Aerotransport *S A André* to British Airways G-AERX
SE-AFA	5614	AB Aerotransport *Svealand*; to AB Skandinavisk Flygtransport
SE-AFB	5620	AB Aerotransport *Götaland*; to Svensk Flygtjänst; to Iberia EC-ADO
SE-AFC	5633	AB Aerotransport *Norrland*; to Svensk Flygtjänst; to Iberia EC-ADQ
SE-AFD	5646	AB Aerotransport *Vikingaland*; to Svensk Flygtjänst; to Iberia EC-ADP

Spain

EC-AAF	5851	Iberia *Ebro*	Ex D-AUJA
EC-AAG	5022	Iberia *Tajo*	Ex D-AXUT
EC-AAH	5098	Iberia *Duero*	Ex D-AKYS
EC-AAI	4060	Iberia *La Cierva*	Ex D-AGFD and ZS-AFC
EC-AAJ	4073	Iberia *Guadal Quivir*	Ex D-AVUL
EC-AAK	4076	Iberia	
EC-AAL	7017	Iberia	
EC-AAU	6725	Iberia	Ex EC-CAL
EC-ABD	7053	Iberia	Ex EC-CAJ
EC-ABE	7196	Iberia	Ex EC-CAK
EC-ABF	7220	Iberia	Ex EC-CAN
EC-ABR	5386	Iberia	Ex EC-DAM
EC-ABS	6015	Iberia	Ex EC-DAN
EC-ADO	5620	Iberia	Ex SE-AFB
EC-ADP	5646	Iberia	Ex SE-AFD
EC-ADQ	5633	Iberia	Ex SE-AFC
EC-CAJ	7053	Iberia	Re-registered EC-ABD
EC-CAK	7196	Iberia	Re-registered EC-ABE
EC-CAL	6725	Iberia	Re-registered EC-AAU
EC-CAN	7220	Iberia	Re-registered EC-ABF
EC-DAM	5386	Iberia	Re-registered EC-ABR
EC-DAN	6015	Iberia	Re-registered EC-ABS

Hungary

HA-DUR	5600	Malert *Kiss Jozsef*	later HA-JUC
HA-JUA	5523	Malert	
HA-JUB	5580	Malert	
HA-JUC	5600	Malert	Ex HA-DUR
HA-JUF	6360	Malert	

Uraguay

CX-ABA		CAUSA *Uruguayo*
CX-ABB		CAUSA

Note:

The numbers behind the registration marking indicate the works numbers of the machines. If the line shows further registrations then these are the result of re-registration.

196

Special equipment for Ju 52

Once the Ju 52 was being used for military purposes it became increasingly evident that additional equipment was needed. The first of these cases occurred in 1936, when Ju 52s were used as bombers for Group K88 of the Condor Legion. Defensive armament was adequate for the rear part of the aircraft, but was not practical in the front section. Soviet Polikarpov 1-15 and 1-16 fighters soon recognised this defect and almost invariably attacked from the front. Since completion of modern bombers (Ju 86, Do 17 and He 111) was unlikely before 1937, the commanding officer of 3/K88, Hauptmann Krafft von Delmensingen, had the idea of fitting one rigid front-facing MG17 to the wing surface on each side between fuselage and wing engine. In order to keep drag low the MGs were fitted with cowlings in the shape of hemispheres. Aim was taken from the pilot's seat with the help of an aiming device, which incorporated a speed ring sight, the two MGs being ranged for 450 m intersection. Despite proven success achieved by Krafft von Delmensingen between December 1936 and spring 1937 this idea was not repeated elsewhere. The equipping of a number of Ju 52-3mg3e's belonging to his squadron with gun mountings on the window, on the other hand, was later taken up and implemented at Weserflug. When not in use, the side of the window-mounted gun position was flush with the side of the fuselage so that only the MG15 itself caused additional drag. Angles of firing to the front and rear were in each case 60 degrees from the central position. Of this range 10 degrees of movement was due to the design of the central window (firing angle upwards 60 degrees, downwards 55 degrees). The MGs were fired from a comfortable sitting position.

Experience during the war wth Poland made it advisable to fit a Scarff mounting which permitted firing to the front. The initial version was open; later on Weserflug designed an enclosed version with an acrylic glass dome. The gunner's firing platform was arranged between the seats of pilot and flight engineer. To carry out the replacement of faulty engines as quickly as possible, Weserflug fitted a Ju 52-3m specially for transporting entire engines. A crane with a lifting capacity of 1000 kg was devised for the loading and unloading of engines; it was easy to attach and detach and was fitted laterally on a wing spar and appropriately anchored. The crane was carried in the cabin during flight.

In order to shorten the approach and landing roll two Ju 52-3m's were fitted with ribbon parachutes installed in a container on a plywood platform below the fuselage. Successful tests were carried out by the Luftwaffe test institute at Rechlin. Test results showed that under calm conditions and with a flying weight of 9500 kg, a landing strip of only 150 m was adequate; with wind the distance was even shorter. The landing speed was 135 km/h; with a gross weight of 10000 kg it was 140 km/h. For towing transport gliders by means of a long towing rope Deutsche Forschungsanstalt für Segelflug, the German research institute for gliders, developed a towing device which was attached to the rear end of the Ju 52-3m fuselage. Necessary modifications were carried out by Weserflug. With this towing device up to three transport gliders could be towed, and it proved its efficiency on numerous occasions during 1940/1. During the further course of the war it became apparent that the long towing ropes were not without hazard, since the pilot of the towed aircraft could not ascertain his position vis-á-vis the towing aircraft when visibility was poor. As a result, rigid towing devices were developed. The towed aircraft was connected directly by a rigid shaft to the rear of the Ju 52. Practical tests showed that the flying characteristics were not significantly impaired.

197

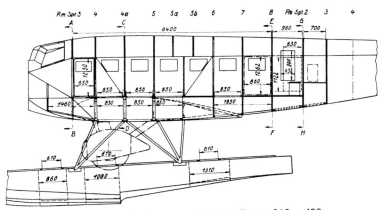

Section A – B		Section C – D		

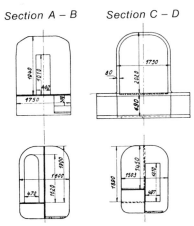

Section E – F   Section G – H

Hatches for luggage holds in floats 610 x 400

Space for power unit   *Space for light luggage between ribs 2 and 3*

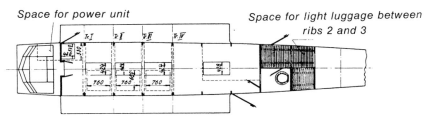

In aircraft fitted with landing gear the hatches for the lower luggage holds are in the floor of the fuselage; in the case of float planes only the hatches in the floor of the payload area are available.

Maximum permissible loads between ribs 3 and 5   400 kg/m²
                              between ribs 5 and 8   350 kg/m²
                         in the lower luggage holds   350 kg/m²

Area	Length mm	Width mm	Height mm	Capacity m³	Remarks
Passenger area approx.	6400	1600	1900	19.6	
Cargo hold rear approx.	960	750	1890	1.4	
Light luggage hold approx.	700	1500	1450 1850	1.7	for aircraft with landing gear only at special request
Cargo hold, front approx.	1460	530	300 670	0.35	partly taken up by power unit
Cargo hold between supports I and II approx.	850	1600	690	1.0	
Cargo hold between supports II and III approx.	850	1600	690	1.0	
Cargo hold between supports III and IV approx.	850	1600	690	1.0	
Cargo hold between ribs 6 and 8 approx.	1850	1220	520	1.2	only for float versions
3 cargo holds each in floats approx.				2.5	

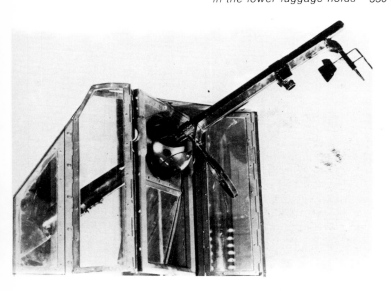

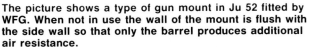

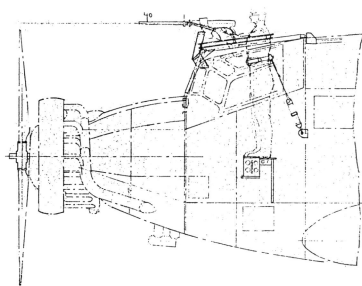

The picture shows a type of gun mount in Ju 52 fitted by WFG. When not in use the wall of the mount is flush with the side wall so that only the barrel produces additional air resistance.
Possible firing angles front and rear 60° from central position. Of these 60°, 10° are due to the design of the central window. (Firing angle upwards 60°, downwards 55°). The MGs were fired from a comfortable sitting position.

Installation of an MG facility in the pilot area of Ju 52/3m. Experience during the war in Poland made it advisable to fit Ju 52/3 m with a circular track which made it possible to shoot in front. The WFG design above is the initial open version. A later development was equipped with an enclosed transparent dome, fitted to all new Ju 52 transport aircraft. The gunner stands between the seats of pilot and flight engineer.

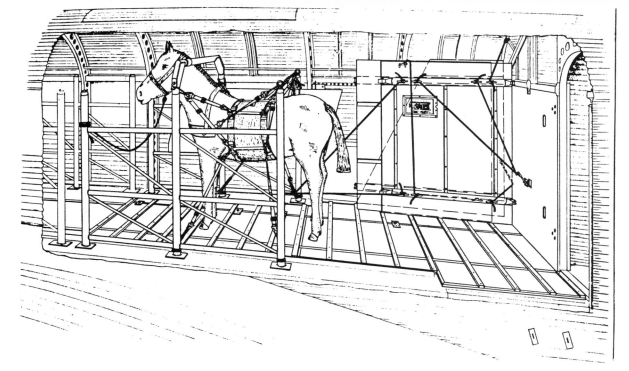

Ju 52 fitted for transporting horses.
It became necessary to devise fittings for transporting a horse in Ju 52 transport planes. The figure above shows that horses could be tied to the standard framework of the aircraft. A new floor cover in the cabin (plywood with roofing felt amd lateral battens) as well as a foldable ramp with similar covering was necessary. The ramp, not shown in the illustration, was carried in the cabin during flight. Apart from loading a horse (weight approx. 450 kg) it was also suitable for loading the following items of equipment

Ammunition cart	600 kg
Mountain artillery 15	630 kg
Half-track motorcycle	1000 kg
Anti-tank gun	437 kg
Infantry gun	570 kg

With the exception of the motorcycle all these items could be loaded in addition to the horse.

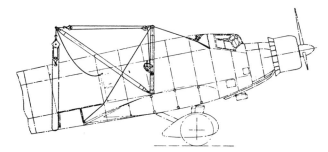

Above: 1 tonne capacity crane for Ju 52/3m (engine transporter). In order to exchange faulty engines as quickly as possible a Ju 52/3 m was fitted for transporting entire engines. A crane with a lifting capacity of 1 tonne was devised for the loading and unloading of engines; it was easy to attach and detach and was fitted laterally on a wing spar and appropriately anchored. The crane was carried in the cabin during flight.
Right: Coupling for long towing rope.

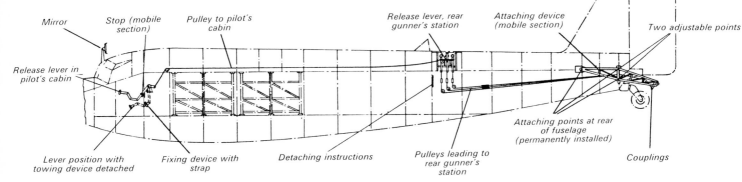

Fittings for Ju 52/3m transport gliders

The illustration shows the devices for attaching towing ropes to the rear end of the fuslage, and the arrangement of pulleys within the fuselage of Ju 52/3 m. The three gliders can be detached simultaneously or consecutively by the towing aircraft. When towing three gliders, each, for example, with a payload of 1300 kg, the travelling speed of the towing aircraft is reduced from around 245 km/h to around 200 km/h.

Rigid towing coupling, Ju 52

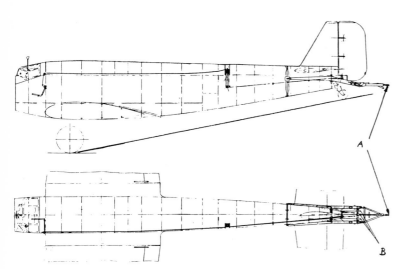

Rigid glider towing device fitted to Ju 52/3 m.

Gliders attached to the towing aircraft by long towing ropes were unable to ascertain their position relative to the towing aircraft, which led to dangerous situations. This disadvantage was avoided by the rigid towing device shown above. The towed glider (only one, however) is attached directly, at point A, without a connecting rope and is therefore immediately behind the towing aircraft. Flight tests showed that this arrangement did not significantly impair the flying characteristics. The design of the towing device, carried out by WFG, also permitted three gliders to be towed in the usual way (towing ropes attached at B) if point A was not used.

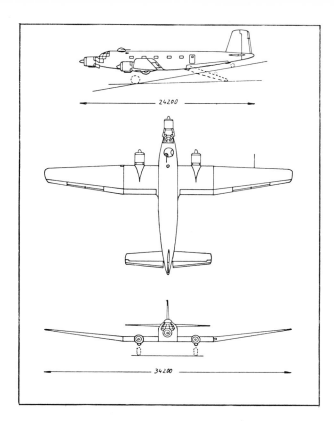

Three views of Ju 352.

24200

34200

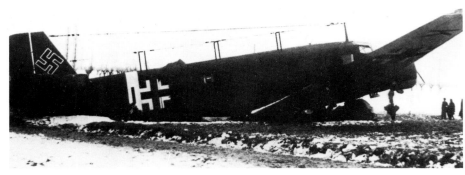

Ju 52-3mg5e with radio jamming installations, Special Command Koch.

Arrangement of aerials on a Ju 52 with radio jamming installations.

Ju 52 fitted as flying test installation: central engine Daimler-Benz DB 600.

Ju 52 fitted as flying test installation: central engine Jumo 211.

Navigational instruction aircraft fitted with special instruments (X-Gerät) for the Luftnachrichten Schul and Versuchsregiment, Köthen 1938, the so-called 'Triple-mast' equipment; this was used to test a VHF precision navigation method for targeted bomb release under conditions of no visibility. KGr100 at Köthen was later moved to Rechlin.

The new arrangement devised by Weserflug still made it possible to tow three gliders by long ropes when the rigid tow was not used. In 1941, before the start of the campaign in Russia, Weserflug was instructed to fit Ju 52-3m's for transporting horses. The horse was attached to the standard framework. In addition, new flooring had to be provided in the cabin (plywood and roofing felt with battens) and a foldable loading ramp with a similar cover. This ramp was carried in the cabin during the flight. As a result of these fittings it was possible to carry not only a horse (weight approx. 450 kg) but many additional loads.

Apart from the special equipment mentioned the Ju 52-3m was also equipped with radio jamming devices and was used as a flying test bed. Aircraft jamming stations were mainly used when flying over enemy territory, either to make it more difficult for one's own unit to be located by radar, or to eliminate the enemy's information activities. In 1941, during the Battle of Britain, it had become apparent that British night fighters fitted with radar installations inflicted painful losses on German bombers. A number of jamming installations were developed which were tested in Ju 52s, by, among others, Special Commando Koch. In July 1942, eight jamming transmitters were fitted into a Ju 52. This took off from Catania before attack by Luftflotte 2 on Malta in Spring 1942, and circled halfway between Sicily and Malta in order to interfere with British radar installations. Later, other aircraft types were also fitted with these jamming devices.

To test new engines, the central engines of a number of Ju 52s were replaced by new engines to be tested under flight conditions. These machines belonged to the Luftwaffe test station at Rechlin. Aircraft used in tests there included Ju 52 GS + AR, GS + AQ and CG + QQ using Daimler-Benz DB 605A and E, Jumo 213 and Jumo 222 engines. These flying test beds were used as late as the beginning of 1945 and always

proved successful.

A number of aircraft belonging to the series Ju 52-3mg4e were refitted as 'Flying Lecture Theatre' aircraft. These were used for a variety of instructional purposes, in particular for training wireless operators and observers. Depending on their use, all necessary radio and direction-finding equipment was installed. Because of the favourable experience had by the Luftwaffe with this type of instructional aircraft, Switzerland also ordered three machines for this purpose.

Aircraft markings
The following list does not claim to be complete and cannot be completed, since numerous documents were destroyed at the end of the war. It is simply an attempt to give, on the basis of extensive compilation work, a view of production data of Ju 52s in Germany. Wherever possible total losses have been marked by (+). It would appear that only 81 machines of the first series 4000 were built. Series 1000, 2000, 3000 and the 6-digit works number series were probably built after series 7000.

Works number	First registration	Additional registration	Remarks
4001	D-1974	D-UZYP	Ju 52 be
4002	D-2133	D-USUS	Ju 52 ci
4003		D-USON	Ju 52 ce
4004	D-2317	SE-ADEM, D-UBES	Ju 52 ce
4005	D-2356		Ju 52 cai, + 27.5.33
4006	CF-ARM		Ju 52 ce, cao
4007		D-UHYF	Ju 52 ce

Works number	First registration	Additional registration	Remarks
4008	Juan del Valle, Bolivien		Ju 52-3m de
4009	Huanuni, Bolivien		Ju 52-3m de
4010	621 Kolumbien		Ju 52-3m di
4011	622 Kolumbien		Ju 52-3m di
4012	623 Kolumbien		Ju 52-3m di
4013	D-2201	D-ADOM Boelcke	Ju 52-3m ce (Reichsbahn)
4014	OH-ALK	OH-LAK Sampo	Ju 52-3m di
4015	D-2202	D-ADYL Richthofen	Ju 52-3m ce
4016	CV-FAI	YR-ABF	Ju 52-3m ba
4017	SE-ADR	Södermanland	Ju 52-3m ce
4018	Chorolque	Bolivien	Ju 52-3m de
4019	D-2468	D-AFIR	Ju 52-3m ce (Reichsbahn)
4020	D-2490	D-AFYS Gustav Dörr	Ju 52-3m fe +1941
4021	D-2600	D-AHUT Immelmann/Buddecke	Ju 52-3m fes +1941
4022	D-2527	D-AGUK M.v.Richthofen/Kurt Wolff	Ju 52-3m fes +1942
4023	D-2526	D-AGAF Zephir	Ju 52-3m fe
4024	PP-CAT	Anhanga	Ju 52-3m fe
4025	D-2588	D-AHIH Rudolf Kleine	Ju 52-3m fe +1941
4026	D-2624	D-AJAN Rudolf Berthold	Ju 52-3m fe +1941
4027	D-2640	D-AZEV	Ju 52-3m fe
4028	D-2649	D-AJUX Göring/U. Neckel	Ju 52-3m fe
4029	D-2650	D-AKEP Fritz Rumey	Ju 52-3m fe +1942
4030	D-2725	D-AKOK Paul Bäumer	Ju 52-3m fe +1942
4031	D-2759		
4032			
4033	D-3012	D-AHIP TK+HB	
4034			
4035	D-3049	D-ALAS H. Gontermann	Ju 52-3m ge
4036	D-3050	D-ALUN K. Wintgens	Ju 52-3m ge +1941
4037	D-3051	D-AMAM K. Wüsthoff	Ju 52-3m ge
4038	PP-CAV	Caicara	Ju 52-3m fe
4039	D-3123	D-ANAL G. Leffers	Ju 52-3m ge +1941
4040	D-3127	D-APAR O. Parschau	Ju 52-3m ge
4041	D-3131	D-ARAM Werner Voss	Ju 52-3m ge
4042	D-3136	PP-CAY Paul Billik/Marimba	Ju 52-3m ge
4043	D-ABIS	PP-CAX Gurupira	Ju 52-3m ge
4044	D-ABAN	Emil Thuy	Ju 52-3m ge
4045	D-ABYF	H. Kirschstein	Ju 52-3m ge
4046	D-ADAL	K. Allmenröder =DERULUFT „Flamingo"	
4047	D-AFER	D-AFES Franz Büchner	Ju 52-3m ge +1942
4048	D-AGIS	W. Schmitt =DERULUFT „Kormoran"	+1941
4049	D-AHUS	H. Kroll =DERULUFT „Milan"	
4050	D-AJIM	H. Göring	Ju 52-3m ge
4051			
4052	D-AXES	Hans Berr	+1941
4053	D-AXAN	D-AHIT Buddecke/Immelmann II	
4054	D-ATON	Erwin Böhme	Ju 52-3m ge +1942
4055	D-AQAR	Walter Höhndorf	Ju 52-3m ho

Works number	First registration	Additional registration	Remarks
4056			
4057	ZS-AFB	Lord Ch. Somerset	Ju 52-3m ge
4058	ZS-AFA	PP-VAL Jan van Riebeeck	Ju 52-3m ge
4049	ZS-AFD	D-ACBO Sir B.d'Urban	Ju 52-3m ge + 1940
4060	ZS-AFC	D-AGFD - EC-AAI	Ju 52-3m ge
4061	Bolivar	Bolivien	
4062	I-BEZI		Ju 52-3m ge
4063	I-BAUS		Ju 52-3m ge
4064	I-BIZI	AI + AC D-AIAO	
4065	D-AHIT		
4066	D-ABAQ	GC+AE Manfred von Richthofen	II + 9. 1. 43
4067			
4068	D-ABIZ	Erich Albrecht	
4069	D-ABIK	Manfred von Richthofen	
4070	D-ADEF	Adolf Schirmer	
4071	D-ANYF	Erich Pust	+ 1941
4072	D-AMIP	Fritz Erb	
4073	D-AVUL	EC-AAJ Bruno Rodschinka	
4074	D-ASIS	Wilhelm Cuno	
4075	D-APEF	PP-CBG Karl Wessel	
4076	OE-LAK	D-AJAT EC-AAK Stoisavlevic	
4077	D-ANOP	LN-DAE Fritz Simon	
4078	PP-CBB	Tupay	
4079	D-APOR	PP-CBF Olaf Bieberstein	
4080	OE-LAM	D-AGDA Wedigo von Froreich	+ 24. 2. 42
4081	LV-AAN		
5005		HK 920	RAF-Beute in Nahost
5010	D-ALAN	Eduard Dostler	+ 1942

Works number	First registration	Additional registration	Remarks
5011	D-ALEF		
5012			
5013			
5014	D-ANOL	Albert Dossenbach	+ 1941
5015			
5016			
5017			
5018	SG + BB	4V + MR	
5019	D-AVIR	Reichsbahn	
5020	D-AZIS	Horst Wessel	
5021	D-AZAN	DB + EX Joachim v. Schröder	
5022	D-AXUT	EC-AAG Lothar v. Richthofen	
5023	D-AXOS	Oswald Boelcke	
5024			
5025			
5026	D-ABES	Hermann Thomsen	+ 1942
5027	RJ + NJ	4V + EC	
5028			
5029			
5030			
5031			
5032			
5033			
5034	D-AHAL	Otto Bernert	
5043	D-ARYS	Hans Kirschstein	
5044	D-ASOR		+ 24. 4. 36 Lechfeld
5053	D-AQUQ	PP-CBR Adolf von Tutscheck	
5055	D-APYX	H4 + AA Reichsbahn	
5056			
5057	KB + AB	4V + KP	
5058			
5059			
5060	D-AMIT	O. V. Beaulieu-Marconnay	
5061			
5062			

Works number	First registration	Additional registration	Remarks
5063			
5064			
5065	D-AJUP	Reichsbahn	
5072	D-ANEN	Fritz Pütter	+1942
5073			
5074	D-APOK	Max v. Müller	
5075			
5076			
5077			
5078	D-ASIH	Rudolf Windisch	
5081		S2+PO9	+25.10.37 Tutow
5089	KG+FV	4V+LS	
5093	D-ALUG		
5096	RK+AV		1945 to RAF: VM 970
5098	D-AKYS	EC-AAH Emil Thuy – Duero	
5100	PP-CBE	Larussu	
5101			
5102	D-ADIP		
5103			
5104	D-AGES	O. Kissenberth	»Eurasia XVII«
5109	D-AMAQ	HC-SND PP-CBH	Max von Mulzer
5115	TK+BJ	4V+DD	
5116			
5117			
5118	BD+PP	4V+DS	
5119			
5120	D-ADER	PP-CBE Hans Wende	
5128	D-ANAZ	Willi Charlett	+1943
5151		S2+P12	+25.10.37 Tutow
5169	D-ATAK	Marschall v. Bieberstein	
5173	DS+AF		
5180	OE-LAR	D-ALYL/NG+VY 1Z+HV »XI. Olympiade Berlin 1936«	
5185	7U+HN	4./TG 20	+7.9.44
5189	D-AXOP		
5195	D-AHEP		

Works number	First registration	Additional registration	Remarks
5219	SE+HT	4V+AS	
5232		TG 20	to RAF 9.10.45
5233	D-APEH		
5234			
5235			
5236			
5237	D-ABON	SG+BC	
5253	GA+WG	4V+ZD	
5261	D-AGST	PP-CAZ	
5267	D-AVUP	Kurt Steidel	
5272	D-AGIQ	D-ASIQ Martin Zander	
5278	D-ADEK	Anton Schulz	
5283	PP-CBA	Aconcagua	
5289	OE-LAL		+16.3.1936
5294	D-AMAK	Volkmar von Arnim	
5320	D-AMEV		
5329	D-ANYK	Wilhelm Schmidt	
5337		Feldluftzeuggr.	+28.11.41 Kristiansd
5339	GD+LV	4V+FU	
5342	VD+XB	4V+BS	
5358	DK+WE	1Z+EV	
5372	D-ASAF	TJ+HZ	
5375		Air Min 104	
5379			2./KGr.zbV. 800
5386	EC+ABR	EC-DAM	
5405		KGr.zbV 108	
5403	DB+QI	4V+PP	
5415		KGr.zbV 108	
5416		S5+C20	
5419	4D+XS		
5429	D-AKIY	LN-KAG William Langanke	
5440	SE-AER	G-AERU Västmanland	
5450	TA+CZ	1Z+CU	
5453	PP-CBC	Guarany	
5455	KQ+MM	1Z+EU	
5459	PP-SPD		
5462	33+K39		+6.4.37 Liegnitz
5463	RC+AR	4V+BC/TG 20	1945 in Norway
5464	DK+TI	4V+CN	

Works number	First registration	Additional registration	Remarks	Works number	First registration	Additional registration	Remarks
5465	PP-SPE	Cidade de Rio de Janeiro		5645	TN+BS		
5470	D-ALAM			5646	SE-AFD	EC-ADP Vikingaland	
5472	D-AGEI	Karl Allmenröder		5656	D-AMYE	PP-CBL Los Andes	
5475	DH+ED	1Z+DT		5658		KGr.zbV 108	
5478	D-AJAO	PP-CBD Robert Weichard		5663	D-ANOY	Rudolf von Thüna	
5484	D-AKUO	Paul Billik	+ 1941	5672	OO-AGW		
5489	D-AQUI	LN-DAH		5673	D-AFAM		
5492	I-ABJZ			5682	D-APUP	Marschall von Bieberstein	
5494	OH-ALL	Kaleva		5685	D-AGAK	Ulrich Neckel	
5499	TN+BQ			5689	PP-SPF	Cidade de Santos	
5502	D-ALUE	Joachim von Schröder		5693	D-AXAT	Rudolf Windisch	+ 1943
5509	KB+HN	4V+CP		5715		VM 985 PH-UBA	
5510	OO-AGU			5727	OE-LAP	D-ATEA Philipp v. Blaschke	
5514	OO-AGV			5734	D-AMEI	Fritz von Röth	
5518	OO-CAP	SE-AES »S.A.André« G-AERX		5740	D-ALAM	Wilhelm Langanke	+ 1943
5523	HA-JUA			5747	D-ANJH	Hans Loeb	
5526			Air service Norway	5748	D-ATAO	Alfred Bauer	
5531	VA-DO	4V+AP		5751	LN-DAI	Hauken	
5537	M3+BA			5760		KGr.zbV 108	+ 7. 11. 42
5555	D-AGOO	Fritz Siman	Supreme Command Norwegian Air Force	5766	RG+NL	1Z+MT	
5575	D-AMOS	TJ++HX		5767	D-AVUP		
5580	HA-JUB			5777	D-ABUR	Charles Haar	
5588	SP-AKX	G-AGAE		5791	SE+IM	SE-AKS	B-Schule Wien.-Neust.
5590	OE-LAN	D-AKEQ SG+BM Gustav Rubritius	+ 1942	5792	ZS-AJII		
5592		4V+CA		5796	IZ-AZ	4V+AN	
5596	7U+OM	4./TG 20	19. 10. 44 + Kirkenes	5797	D-ATYZ	Hans Hackmack	
5600	HA-DUR	HA-JUC Kiss Joszef		5800	D-AFOP	Karl Hochmuth	
5609		KGr.zbV 108	+ 5. 4. 42 Bardufoss	5807	»36«		Ju 52-3m K Austrian Air Force
5610	OY-DAL	Selandia		5809	H4+FL		
5614	SE-AFA	Svealand		5810			KGr.zbV 108, TG 20 to RAF Air service Norway RLM + 7. 11. 42
5620	SE-AFB	EC-ADO Götaland		5815	OO-AUA		
5630	D-AROS			5817	H4+PM		
5633	SE-AFC	EC-ADQ Norrland		5820	»37«		Ju 52-3m K Austrian Air Force
				5824	R 344	LV-AAB Patagonia LV-AAG	Aeroposta Argentina

Works number	First registration	Additional registration	Remarks
5827	OO-AUB		
5829	R 346	LV-AAI	Aeroposta Argentina
5833	R 345	LV-AAH	Aeroposta Argentina
5835	OE-HKA	Austrian Air Force Communications aircraft	
5847	9G+HA		
5851	D-AUJA	EC-AAF	
5852	OO-AUF		
5854	D-AUKE		
5858	D-AUKE		
5860	D-AYHO	Peter Strasser	
5873		4V+BA	
5877	CX-ABA	El Uruguayo	
5881	G-AFAP	Jason	
5885	GS+AY	1Z+LW	
5886	CX-ABB	El Argentino	
5900	SA-BK		
5916	NR+AG	4V+CD	
5919	D-ARDS	Robert Weichard	+ 1942
5930	S-AWBR		
5933	OE-LAS	D-AMFR	
5938	D-AFCD	Erich Albrecht	+ 1941
5940	D-ATDB	Walter Bayer	
5942	D-AUJG	Hans Wende	
5944	M3+CA		
5945	DC+SF	1./KGr.zbV. 108	+ 4. 3. 41 Gardemoen
5948		KGr.zbV 108	
5950	AV+SG	4V+KR	
5954	D-ABVF	Franz Wagner	+ 1942
5962	CR-AAJ	Lourenco Marques	
5965	D-ACBQ	TJ+HY	
5967	CR-AAK	Quelimane	
5970	D-AKCD	TJ+HW	
5973	CR-AAL	Nampula	
5974	P4+CH	Tr.Fl.F.Nord	+ 16. 11. 41
5979	D-ANXG	Hans Kirschstein	+ 1941
5984	SX-ACF	VM-980	
5996		1Z-BS	
6004	SX-ACH		
6005	TJ+HV	4V+FR	
6014	D-ASFD	Heinrich Mathy	
6015	EC-DAN	EC-ABS	
6020	D-AGTC	Wilhelm Cuno	
6032	D-AGTC	KGr.zbV 108	+ 24. 2. 43
6036	OO-AUG		
6042	D-AHMS	Martin Zander	+ 1941
6046	D-ABED	Victor Neubrand	
6047	D-AHFN	H. Krichelsdorf	+ 1942
6048		N9+DA Liaison Squadron Norwegian Air force	
6057	D-AFFQ	Gustav Falke	
6063	00-AUG		
6064			TG 20 to RAF 9. 10. 45
6066	D-ADHF	Walter Höhndorf	+ 1943
6069	7U+OK		4./TG 20 + 21. 10. 44
6086			TG 20 1945 to Norway
6093	D-ALUG	Josef Zauritz	
6101	7U+FK	KGr.zbV 108	+ 5. 11. 42
6122	BF+FW	1Z+CT	
6129	SE+JR	4V+DR/H4+LU	
6132	SE+HU		B-Schule Wien. Neust.
6149	D-APXD	Robert Untucht	+ 1943
6167		9P+FW	
6171	D-ARAD	Volkmar von Arnim	MOK Norway
6176	TD+AH	4V+HN	
6179		H4+BB	
6180	D-ARIW	Joachim Blankenburg	+1941
6190	AH+FP	4V+BN	
6222		M3+EA	
6224	LV-ZBL		
6277			Kgr.zbV 108
6284	SE+PS		
6285	DK+CM	4V+MU	
6290	DA+FL	4V+JP	
6292		H4+CN	
6294			TG 20 to RAF 9. 10. 45
6301		1Z+BM	
6311			Z 2 D Military symbol
6322	TE+HY	1Z+AN / 4V+JS	

Works number	First registration	Additional registration	Remarks	Works number	First registration	Additional registration	Remarks
6343	7U+HK		I./TG 20 +23.10.44	6584		KGr.zbV.108	+10.7.41 Vaasa (Norw.)
6346		KGr.zbV.108	+13.12.41 Fornebu	6585	A-701	HB-HOS	Swiss Air Force
6352		1Z+CR		6595	A-702	HB-HOT	Swiss Air Force
6354	LV-ZBJ						
6360	HA-JUF			6608	TN+BX		
6367		1Z+MM		6610	A-703	HB-HOP	Swiss Air Force
6369	D-ASLG	Alfred Viereck	+1942				
6370	D-AVAJ	Olaf Bielenstein	+1941	6622	TS+BT	4V+ES	
6372	D-AXFH	H.E.Lochner	+1942	6625	CW+AC	4V+DP	
6385	D-ABFA	TT+LN Otto Parschau	+1941	6650	D-ADBW	Emil Thuy	
				6657	CA+JY		
6386	D-AGEP	Adolf v. Tutscheck	+1942	6659	D-AGBI	Max v. Mulzer	+1942
6387	D-ADBO	O. v. Beaulieu-Marc.	+1941	6664	SE+KC	SE-AKR	
6393		4D+XB		6670	D-AEAO	Rudolf Fritsche	+1941
6395		Flugber.L.Fl.5	+11.11.42	6682	CK+BA	4V+MS	
6399	7U+GM	I./TG 20	+23.10.44	6710	I-BIOS	AS+PI	
6401	D-AEBT		Fl. Prüfstd. f. DB 603 A	6716			2./TG 20 +18.11.1943
6403	LV-ZBF			6724		7U+CK	KGr.zbV 108 to RAF 9.10.45
6410	OO-AUK						
6422	VB+PY	4V+ZW		6725	EC-CAL	EC-AAU	
6432	D-ABEW	Rudolf v. Thüna	+1943	6734	D-APGU	Bruno Rodschinka	
6442	D-AREB	Charles Haar		6738	BA+KM	KGr.zbV 106	Wreck in Sweden 1941
6451	DM+WV	1Z+BD		6748	CN+BW	4V+KS	
6452	D-AGOB	Hans Handke	27.6.1941	6750	D-APZX	R. Stiljevic	VM 908 G-AHBP
6456		7U+AM	Emergency landing Sweden +1946 Tr.Fl.St. Norway	6751	DC+SP		Shot down by Swedish anti-aircraft guns.
6474	CF+GW			6753	..+DO		
6482	TF+HB	1Z+DN 4V+GN		6754			Shot down by Swedish anti-aircraft guns.
6492	BA+LQ	1Z+JU		6755			KGr.zbV 108 +27.6.41
6510	PP-SPH	PP-DZY		6757			Wekusta 5 +3.12.41
6527		TG 20	1945 to Norway				
6550	D-ACBE	Emil Schäfer	+1943	6765	I-BOAN	AI+AT	
6558	NC+OZ	4V+MN		6775	D-AHGA	Paul Billik	
6561	D-AWAS	Joachim Blankenburg		6779	D-ARCK	Van Vloten	
6562			Courier Service Lapland	6780			1945 to Norway
				6790	D-ARYU	Hans Wende	
6567	D-AGAC		1945 in England	6798	CO+BP	1Z+EW	

Works number	First registration	Additional registration	Remarks
6800	D-AHGB	PP-CBP Rudolf Kleine	
6803	I-BERO	AS+PE	
6804			Transport Flights North + 22.4.42
6821	VB+UP		
6837			Flight Intelligence Unit 5 + 23.3.42
6844	7U+GK		I./TG 20 + 23.10.44
6867		M3+FA	
6873		7U+JK	2./TGR.20 abger. Gardemoen
6906	CF+KB	4V+KW	
6929			1./KGr.zbV 108 + 1.1.41
6932			1./KGr.zbV 108 + 2.1.41
6933			KGr.zbV 108
6935	DR+WC		
6936		1Z+AS	
6940			KGr.zbV 108 + 2.11.41
6942		H4+IL 8A+BK	Sea Transport Norway
6948	DR+WP		1./KGr.zbV 108 + 4.1.42
6950		9P+EL	2./KGr.zbV 108 + 17.6.42
6957			KGr.zbV 108 + 24.2.43
6968			KGr.zbV 108 + 8.10.41
6978	7U+FH		KGr.zbV 108 + 5.11.42
6993	D-AEHP	PB+KA	
7000	TE+EL	1Z+FU	
7009			2.Sea Transport + 17.11.43
7014	VC+ZP	4V+GR	
7015	VC+ZQ	4V+JR	
7017	EC-AAL		
7018	VC+ZW		
7029	D-APAJ	Erich Rist	
7044	D-ABAN		

Works number	First registration	Additional registration	Remarks
7047	KB+RE	4V+EN	
7048	KB+RF		
7049	KB+RH		
7050	KB+RI		
7051	KB+RJ	1Z+LV	
7053	EC-CAJ	EL-ABD	
7077	D-ASDi	Rudolf Kleine	
7089	D-ASHY	Gustav Doerr	
7094	DD+ZM	1Z+GU	
7095	DD+ZN		
7096	DD+ZO	1Z+BT	
7097	DD+ZP		
7098	DD+ZQ		
7100		9P+HK	
7132	DE-TV		
7147	KD+IN	7U+IL 4V+DC	10./TGr.4 + 6.11.44
7160	D-ATAW	Lothar v. Richthofen	
7170			KGr.zbV 108
7172	D-AUXZ	O. v. Beaulieu-Marconnay	+ 1941
7196	EC-CAK	EC-ABE	
7208	D-AYGX	Johannes Höroldt	+ 1942
7210	CE+GH		
7215	CE+GM	LN+KAH	T.Gr.20
7220	EC-CAN	EC-ABF	
7229	8A+..	LN-KAB	Sea Transport 2 Norwegen »Tyrihans«
7244	D-AIAG	Olaf Bielenstein	
7250	GA+WV		
7251	GA+WW		
7252	GA+WX		
7253	GA+WY		
7254	GA+WZ		
7256	D-AVIU	OH-LAM Theodor Schöpwinkel 1.(F)/22	SE-BUE VH-BUU
7258			
7268	D-AIAH	Karl Hochmuth	
7274	S 17+M55		
7279	TG+ES	4V+BP	
7280	TG+ET		
7281	TG+EU		
7282	TG+EV		

Works number	First registration	Additional registration	Remarks	Works number	First registration	Additional registration	Remarks
7283	TG+EW			7357	NJ+KF		
7284	TG+EX			7358	NJ+KG		
7285	TG+EY			7359	NJ+KH		
7286	TG+EZ			7360	NJ+KI		
7287	DG+SA			7361	NJ+KJ		
7288	DG+SB			7362	NJ+KK		
7289	DG+SC			7363	NJ+KL		
7290	DG+SD			7364	NJ+KM		
7291	DG+SE	1Z+DU		7365	NJ+KN		
7292	DG+SF			7366	NJ+KO		
7293	DG+SG			7367	NJ+KP		
7294	DG+SH			7368	NJ+KQ		
7295	DG+SI			7369	NJ+KR		
7296	DG+SJ	4V+MT		7370	NJ+KS		
7297	DG+SK	4V+CS		7371	NJ+KT		
7298	DG+SL			7372	NJ+KU	4V+BR	
7299	DG+SM			7373	NJ+KV		
7329	NK+MO	1Z+MW		7374	NJ+KW		
7331	BV+OF	4V+LW		7375	NJ+KX	KGr.zbV 300	
7332	BV+OG			7376	NJ+KY		
7333	BV+OH			7377	NJ+KZ		
7334	BV+OI		1945 to Norway				
7335	BV+OJ			7380			
7336	BV+OK			7381	VK+PA		
7337	BV+OL			7382	VK+PB		
7338	BV+OM			7383	VK+PC		
7339	BV+ON		1945 to Norway	7384	VK+PD		
7340	BV+OO			7385	VK+PE	4V+LP	
7341	BV+OP			7386	VK+PF		
7342	BV+OQ			7387	VK+PG		
7343	BV+OR			7388	VK+PH		
7344	BV+OS			7389	VK+PI		
7345	BV+OT			7390	VK+PJ		
7346	BV+OU			7391	VK+PK		
7347	BV+OV			7392	VK+PL		
7348	BV+OW			7393	VK+PM		
7349	BV+OX			7394	VK+PN		
7350	BV+OY			7395	VK+PO	4V+EW	
7351	BV+OZ	4V+EP		7396	VK+PP		
7352	NJ+KA			7397	VK+PQ		
7353	NJ+KB			7398	VK+PR		
7354	NJ+KC			7399	VK+PS		
7355	NJ+KD			7400	VK+PT	1Z+MW	
7356	NJ+KE			7401	VK+PU		
				7402	VK+PV		
				7403	VK+PW		

Works number	First registration	Additional registration	Remarks	Works number	First registration	Additional registration	Remarks
7404	VK+PX			7572	DG+KV		
7405	VK+PY			7573	DG+KW		
7406	VK+PZ			7574	DG+KX		
7407	SN+FA			7575	DG+KY		
7408	SN+FB			7576	DG+KZ		
7409	SN+FC			7577	NG+GA		
7410	SN+FD			7578	NG+GB		
7411	SN+FE			7579	NG+GC		
7412	SN+FF			7580	NG+GD		
7413	SN+FG			7581	NG+GE		
7414	SN+FH	4V+GD		7582	NG+GF		
				7583	NG+GG		
7480	CK+QD	1Z+BD		7584	NG+GH		
7481	CK+QE			7585	NG+GI		
7482	CK+QF			7586	NG+GJ		
7483	CK+QG	4V+FN		7587	NG+GK		
7485	CK+QI	TG 20		7588	NG+GL		
7490	OH-LAP	Petsamo		7589	NG+GM		
7493	OH+LAO	Waasa		7590	NG+GN		
		SE-BUD,		7591	NG+GO		
		VH-BUV,		7592	NG+GP		
		VH-GSS		7593	NG+GQ	4V+AR	
7504	DP+ED	4V+DN		7601	DI+KA		
7529	DP+BZ	1Z+CD		7602	DI+KB		
7544	KA+SN	1Z+DV		7603	DI+KC		
7551	DG+KA			7604	DI+KD		
7552	DG+KB			7605	DI+KE		
7553	DG+KC			7606	DI+KF		
7554	DG+KD	4V+DU		7607	DI+KG	4V+BT	
7555	DG+KE			7608	DI+KH		
7556	DG+KF			7609	DI+KI		
7557	DG+KG			7610	DI+KJ		
7558	DG+KH			7611	DI+KK		
7559	DG+KI			7612	DI+KL		
7560	DG+KJ			7613	DI+KM	4V+GT	
7561	DG+KK			7614	DI+KN		
7562	DG+KL			7615	DI+KO		
7563	DG+KM			7616	DI+KP		
7564	DG+KN			7617	DI+KQ		
7565	DG+KO			7618	DI+KR		
7566	DG+KP			7619	DI+KS		
7567	DG+KQ			7620	DI+KT		
7568	DG+KR			7621	DI+KU		
7569	DG+KS			7622	DI+KV		
7570	DG+KT			7623	DI+KW		
7571	DG+KU			7624	DI+KX		

Works number	First registration	Additional registration	Remarks	Works number	First registration	Additional registration	Remarks
7625	DI+KY			7671	GG+FS		
7626	DI+KZ			7672	GG+FT		
7627	DM+WA	4V+ET		7673	GG+FU		
7628	DM+WB			7674	GG+FV		
7629	DM+WC			7675	GG+FW		
7630	DM+WD			7676	GG+FX		
7631	DM+WE			7677	GG+FY		
7632	DM+WF			7678	GG+FZ		
7633	DM+WG			7679	GL+KA	4V+EY	
7634	DM+WH			7680	GL+KB		
7635	DM+WI			7681	GL+KC		
7636	DM+WJ			7682	GL+KD		
7637	DM+WK			7683	GL+KE	1Z+LT	
7638	DM+WL			7684	GL+KF		
7639	DM+WM			7685	GL+KG		
7640	DM+WN			7686	GL+KH		
7641	DM+WO	4V+GW		7687	GL+KI		
7642	DM+WP			7688	GL+KJ		
7643	DM+WQ			7689	GL+KK		
7644	DM+WR			7690	GL+KL		
7645	DM+WS			7691	GL+KM		
7646	DM+WT			7692	GL+KN		
7647	DM+WU			7693	GL+KO		
7648	DM+WV			7694	GL+KP		
7649	DM+WW			7695	GL+KQ		
7650	DM+WX			7696	GL+KR		
7651	DM+WY			7697	GL+KS		
7652	DM+WZ			7698	GL+KT	1Z+CV	
7653	GG+FA			7725	DF+ZY	1Z+AW	
7654	GG+FB	4V+LV		7726	DF+ZZ		
7655	GG+FC			7727	DL+KA	1Z+AU	
7656	GG+FD			7728	DL+KB		
7657	GG+FE			7729	DL+KC		
7658	GG+FF			7730	DL+KD		
7659	GG+FG			7731	DL+KE	1Z+BU	
7660	GG+FH			7732	DL+KF		
7661	GG+FI			7733	DL+KG		
7662	GG+FJ			7734	DL+KH		
7663	GG+FK			7735	DL+KI		
7664	GG+FL			7736	DL+KJ		
7665	GG+FM			7737	DL+KK		
7666	GG+FN			7738	DL+KL		
7667	GG+FO			7739	DL+KM		
7668	GG+FP			7740	DL+KN		
7669	GG+FQ			7741	DL+KO		
7670	GG+FR			7742	DL+KP		

Works number	First registration	Additional registration	Remarks	Works number	First registration	Additional registration	Remarks
7743	DL+KQ			3007	BJ+YH		
7744	DL+KR			3008	BJ+YI		
7745	DL+KS			3009	BJ+YJ		
7746	DL+KT	1Z+ED		3010	BJ+YK		
7747	DL+KU			3011	BJ+YL		
7748	DL+KV	1Z+JV		3012	BJ+YM		
7749	DL+KW			3013	BJ+YN		
7750	DL+KX			3014	BJ+YO		
7751	DL+KY			3015	BJ+YP		
7752	DL+KZ			3016	BJ+YQ		
1301	D-AZIR	Fritz Erb		3017	BJ+YR	4V+MP	
1332		1Z+FW		3018	BJ+YS		
1334	BD+BP			3019	BJ+YT		
1368	D-ADUE	TK+HA		3020	BJ+YU		
1372		G6+CA		3021	BJ+YV		
2803	TS+PJ	4V+KR		3022	BJ+YW		
2810	DK+NT	1Z+FT		3023	BJ+XY		
2820	D-AGEQ			3024	BJ+YY		
2821	D-AFOX			3025	BJ+YZ		
2826	KI+AK			3026	BR+AA		
2827		KGr.zbV 108		3027	BR+AB		
2833	D-ATYS		Hospital aircraft	3028	BR+AC		
2839	AR+EA	4V+LT		3029	BR+AD		
2852	TM+BY			3030	BR+AE		
2863	7U+IK	2./KGr.zbV 108	+ 22.5.43	3031	BR+AF		
2892	NI+NF			3032	BR+AG		
2899		KGr.zbV 108	+ 27.9.42	3033	BR+AH		
2925		T.Gr.20	+ 25.12.43	3034	BR+AI		
2931		KGr.zbV 108	+ 11.4.42	3035	BR+AJ	4V+HT	
2938		KGr.zbV. 108	25.9.41 Kiel-Holtenau	3036	BR+AK		
				3037	BR+AL		
2942	NN+CA	1Z+DW		3038	BR+AM		
2977/ 1330	NO+IJ		24.2.43 Emergency landing in Sweden	3039	BR+AN		
				3040	BR+AO		
				3041	BR+AP		
2982	7U+PK	KGr.zbV 108		3042	BR+AQ		
2998		VN 742 G-AHOK		3043	BR+AR		
3000	BJ+YA			3044	BR+AS		
3001	BJ+YB			3045	BR+AT		
3002	BJ+YC		Hospital aircraft	3046	BR+AU		
3003	BJ+YD		to RAF 28.10.45	3047	BR+AV		
3004	BJ+YE			3048	BR+AW		
3005	BJ+YF			3049	BR+AX		
3006	BJ+YG			3050	BR+AY		
				3051	BR+AZ		
				3052	KF+UA		

Works number	First registration	Additional registration	Remarks	Works number	First registration	Additional registration	Remarks
3053	KF+UB			3123	KQ+CU	4V+ER	
3054	KF+UC			3124	KQ+CV		
3055	KF+UD			3125	KQ+CW		
3056	KF+UE			3126	KQ+CX		
3057	KF+UF			3127	KQ+CY		
3058	KF+UG			3128	KQ+CZ		
3059	KF+UH			3139	BC+RA		
3060	KF+UI			3140	BC+RB		
3061	KF+UK			3141	BC+RC		
3062	KF+UL			3142	BC+RD		
3063	KF+UM			3143	BC+RE		
3064	KF+UN			3144	BC+RF		
3065	KF+UO			3145	BC+RG		
3066	KF+UP			3146	BC+RH		
3067	KF+UQ			3147	BC+RI		
3068	KF+UR	4V+HS KGr.zbV 300		3148	BC+RJ		
				3149	BC+RK		
3069	KF+US			3150	BC+RL		
3070	KF+UT			3151	BC+RM		
3071	KF+UU			3152	BC+RN		
3072	KF+UV			3153	BC+RO		
3073	KF+UW			3154	BC+RP		
3074	KF+UX			3155	BC+RQ		
3075	KF+UY			3156	BC+RR		
3076	KF+UZ			3157	BC+RS		
3103	KQ+CA			3158	BC+RT		
3104	KQ+CB			3159	BC+RU		
3105	KQ+CC			3160	BC+RV		
3106	KQ+CD			3161	BC+RW		
3107	KQ+CE			3162	BC+RX		
3108	KQ+CF			3163	BC+RY		
3109	KQ+CG			3164	BC+RZ		
3110	KQ+CH			3165	BJ+EA		
3111	KQ+CI			3166	BJ+EB		
3112	KQ+CJ			3167	BJ+EC		
3113	KQ+CK			3168	BJ+ED		
3114	KQ+CL			3169	BJ+EE		
3115	KQ+CM			3170	BJ+EF		
3116	KQ+CN			3171	BJ+EG		
3117	KQ+CO			3172	BJ+EH		
3118	KQ+CP			3173	BJ+EI		
3119	KQ+CQ			3174	BJ+EJ		
3120	KQ+CR			3175	BJ+EK		
3121	KQ+CS			3176	BJ+EL		
3122	KQ+CT			3177	BJ+EM		

Works number	First registration	Additional registration	Remarks	Works number	First registration	Additional registration	Remarks
3178	BJ+EN			3224	PH+OH		
3179	BJ+EO			3225	PH+OI		
3180	BJ+EP			3226	PH+OJ		
3181	BJ+EQ			3227	PH+OK	4V+GS	
3182	BJ+ER			3228	PH+OL		
3183	BJ+ES			3229	PH+OM		
3184	BJ+ET			3230	PH+ON		
3185	BJ+EU			3231	PH+OO		
3186	BJ+EV			3232	PH+OP		
3187	BJ+EW			3233	PH+OQ	4V+DV	
3188	BJ+EX			3234	PH+OR		
3189	BJ+EY			3235	PH+OS		
3190	BJ+EZ			3236	PH+OT		
3191	PD+KA			3237	PH+OU		
3192	PD+KB			3238	PH+OV		
3193	PD+KC			3239	PH+OW		
3194	PD+KD			3240	PH+OX		
3195	PD+KE			3241	PH+OY		
3196	PD+KF			3242	PH+OZ		
3197	PD+KG						
3198	PD+KH			3257		8A+AK/LN-KAI	KGr.zbV 108
3199	PD+KI			3280	TH+UL	4V+KV	
3200	PD+KJ	4V+FS		3292	KI+LA		
3201	PD+KK			3293	KI+LB		
3202	PD+KL			3294	KI+LC	4V+AU	
3203	PD+KM			3295	KI+LD	4V+CC	
3204	PD+KN			3296	KI+LE		
3205	PD+KO			3297	KI+LF		
3206	PD+KP			3298	KI+LG		
3207	PD+KQ			3299	KI+LH		
3208	PD+KR			3300	KI+LI		
3209	PD+KS			3301	KI+LJ	4V+JN	1945 to Norway
3210	PD+KT						
3211	PD+KU			3302	KI+LK		
3212	PD+KV			3303	KI+LL		
3213	PD+KW			3304	KI+LM		
3214	PD+KX			3305	KI+LN		
3215	PD+KY			3306	KI+LO		
3216	PD+KZ			3307	KI+LP		
3217	PH+OA			3308	KI+LQ		
3218	PH+OB			3309	KI+LR		
3219	PH+OC			3310	KI+LS		
3220	PH+OD			3311	KI+LT		
3221	PH+OE			3312	KI+LU		
3222	PH+OF			3313	KI+LV		
3223	PH+OG			3314	KI+LW		

Works number	First registration	Additional registration	Remarks	Works number	First registration	Additional registration	Remarks
3315	KI+LX			130520	CL+KT		
3316	KI+LY			130521	CL+KU	1Z+GT	
3317	KI+LZ	VM 979/G-AHOG		130522	CL+KV	1Z+HW	
3318	PI+PA			130523	CL+KW		
3319	PI+PB			130524	CL+KX		
3320	PI+PC			130525	CL+KY		
3321	PI+PD			130526	CL+KZ		
3322	PI+PE			130527	CT+EA		
3323	PI+PF			130528	CT+EB	1Z+GV	
3324	PI+PG	4V+CR		130529	CT+EC	1Z+HT	
3325	PI+PH			130530	CT+ED		
3326	PI+PI			130531	CT+EE		
3327	PI+PJ			130532	CT+EF		
3328	PI+PK			130533	CT+EG		
3329	PI+PL			130534	CT+EH		
3330	PI+PM			130535	CT+EI		
3331	PI+PN			130704	LN-KAE	PAL	
3332	PI+PO			130712	LN+KAD	Per ex See-Tr. St. 2 Norway	
3333	PI+PP			130714	LN+KAF	Askeladden See-Tr. St. 2 Norway	
3334	PI+PQ						
3335	PI+PR			130731	TC-PEK	Delvet Hava Yollari Turkey	
3336	PI+PS			130732	TC-RUH	Delvet Hava Yollari Turkey	
3337	PI+PT			130761	TC-SEL	Delvet Hava Yollari Turkey	
3338	PI+PU			130862	TC-TEZ	Delvet Hava Yollari Turkey	
3339	PI+PV			130871	TC-ULU	Delvet Hava Yollari Turkey	
3340	PI+PW			130740		an RAF 28. 10. 45	
3341	PI+PX						
3342	PI+PY			131150		VN 740 G-AHOD	
3343	PI+PZ			10002			Field workshop
3344	PK+RA						
3345	PK+RB			10004	NI+MS	1Z+KW	
3346	PK+RC			10018	NI+MQ	4V+BV	
3347	PK+RD	1Z+ET		10064			1945 to Norway
3367	BG+YQ	1Z+CW					
3376		VM 928		10148	RO+SV	1Z+KV	
3401	3K+MK		2. MS- Group	180342	RO+SZ	1Z+BW	
3412		VM 932		180348	NP+YF	1Z+KU	
3428		VM 927/PH-UBB		180349	NP+YG	1Z+AD	
3443	3K+BK		2. MS- Group to RAF 28. 10. 45	180350	NP+YH		
				180351	NP+YI	1Z+MU	
				500116	GN+OU		
3448	3K+KK		2. MS- Group to RAF 9. 10. 45	500138		VN 756 G-AHOJ	
				500146	JU+BM	Landed in Sweden, 27.8.45 to USSR	
3459	PR+YG	1Z+AV					
130519	CL+KS	1Z+DD					

Works number	First registration	Additional registration	Remarks
501191			1945 to Norway
501195			to RAF 28.10.45
501196		7U+IK TG 20,	1945 to Norway Portugal
501198		8A+CK See-Tr.St.2	1945 to Norway
501219		7U+.. 2./TGr.20	1945 to Norway
501358		7U+NL 3./TGr.20	1945 to Norway
501441		VM 923 G-AHOC	
5210078		VN 743 PH-UBC	
640066		7U+AK 2./TGr.20	to RAF 9.10.45 VM 906
640185		Fl.Fü. Norwegen	+18.11.43
640401		TGr.20	1945 to Norway

Works number	First registration	Additional registration	Remarks
640416	DF+FJ		2.5.45 to Sweden
640604		T.Gr.20	to RAF 28.20.45 ??!
640605	D-ADQU	Karl Noack	
640608	D-ADQV	Hermann Stache	
640610	D-ADQW	Harry Rother	
640758		T.Gr.20	to RAF 9.10.45
640994		T.Gr.20	to RAF 28.10.45
641007		T.Gr.20	1945 to Norway
641038	D-AUAV		
641039	D-AUAW		
641040	D-AUAX		
641213		VN 741 G-AHOL	
641227		VN 744 G-AHOI	
641364		VN 746 G-AHOH	
641375	OY-DFU	SE-AYB, VH-BUW, VH-GSW	

Luftwaffe Transport Units eqipped with Junkers Ju 52-3m aircraft

K.G.z.b.V.1 – T.G.1

I./K.G.z.b.V.1 – I./T.G.1

II./K.G.z.b.V.1 – II./T.G.1

III./K.G.z.b.V.1 – III./T.G.1

IV./K.G.z.b.V.1 – IV./T.G.1

K.G.z.b.V.2 – T.G.2

K.Gr.z.b.V.101

K.Gr.z.b.V.102 – III./T.G.3

K.Gr.z.b.V.103

K.Gr.z.b.V.104

K.Gr.z.b.V.105 – IV./T.G.4

K.Gr.z.b.V.106 – III./T.G.2

K.Gr.z.b.V. 107

K.Gr.z.b.V.108 – T.Gr.20

I./K.G.z.b.V.172 – IV./T.G.3

II./K.G.z.b.V.172

K.Gr.z.b.V.9 – I./T.G.3

K.Gr.z.b.V.11

K.Gr.z.b.V.12

K.Gr.z.b.V.50 – II./T.G.3

K.Gr.z.b.V.40

K.Gr.z.b.V.60

Air Transport Unit:

Maritime Air Transport Squadron:

K.Gr.z.b.V.300

K.Gr.z.b.V.400 – III./T.G.4

K.Gr.z.b.V.500 – I./T.G.4

K.Gr.z.b.V.600

K.Gr.z.b.V.700 – LeO 451

K.Gr.z.b.V.800 – II./T.G.2

K.Gr.z.b.V.900

K.Gr.z.b.V.999

K.Gr.z.b.V.5 – T.Gr.30

K.Gr.z.b.V.6

K.Gr.z.b.V.7

K.Gr.z.b.V.8

Army Postal Service K.Gr.z.b.V.S7
K.Gr.z.b.V.S 11
K.Gr.z.b.V. S 13
K.Gr.z.b.V. Frankfurt
K.Gr.z.b.V. Wittstock
K.Gr.z.b.V. Posen
K.Gr.z.b.V. Oels

T.G.1 Ju 52
T.G.2 Ju 52
T.G.3 Ju 52
T.G.4 Ju 52

L.L.G.1
I./L.L.G.1
II./L.L.G.1
III./L.L.G.1
L.L.G.2
I./L.L.G.2
II./L.L.G.2

Note:
As far as it is known only the following transport units had military aircaft markings:

KGzbV1/TGI	1 Z + ..
KGrzbV106/III/TG2	4 V + ..
1/KGrzbV172/IV/TG3	4 V + ..
KGrzbV400/III/Tg 4	4 F + ..
Air transport squadron (Sea)	G 6 + .. (also 8 A + ..)
Transport unit 20	7 V + ..

Ju 53-3m's which landed in Sweden 1939 to 1945

14.4.1940	Ju 52-3m	1Z + BC Staff II/ KGzbV1	Navigational error, landed at Mariestad (Vänern) Return 23.1.41.
14.4.1940	Ju 52-3m	SE + H	Navigational error, shot down by Swedish anti-aircraft guns. Completely wrecked, shot down near Uddevalla.
14.4.1940	Ju 52-3m	SE + HU Works no. 6132 B-School	Navigational error, returned 2.9.40 as SE-AKT. Landed near Grebbestad.
16.4.1940	Ju 52-3m	SE + IM Works no. 5791 B-School	Landed near Grums. Navigational error, returned 2.9. as SE-AKS.
17.4.1940	Ju 52-3m	SE + KC Works no. 6664	Navigational error, landed near Vallsta (ARBRô), returned 2.9. as SE-AKR.
20.5.1940	Ju 52-3m	BA + KM Works no. 6738 KGzbV 108	Returned 11.6.41. Crashed, wreck found 1941.
2.6.1940	Ju 52-3m	DC + SP	Navigational error? Shot down by Swedish anti-aircraft guns over the border.
6.6.1940	Ju 52-3m		Navigational error. Shot down by Swedish anti-aircraft guns near Strömstad.
8.10.41	Ju 52-3m	N9 + AA Courier Squadron	Emergency landing near Vansbro returned 9.10.41.
2.11.1941	Ju 52-3m	P4 + HH	Emergency landing as a result of engine failure near Arjäng, returned 7.11.

13.12.1941	Ju 52-3m		Emergency landing near Gälli-vara, returned 20.12.
29.5.1942	Ju 52-3m	IZ + IX 13/TG 1	Engine failure. Returned 13.6 after repair work at Bulltofta.
24.2.1943	Ju 52-3m g4e	NO + IJ Works no. 2977/ 1330	Courier aircraft. Emergency landing near Lekvattnet; scrapped 1949.
19.7.1943	Ju 52-3m	JU + AM Works no. 6456	Emergency landing because of engine failure, scrapped 1946.
8.5.1945	Ju 52-3m R 12	JU + BM Works no. 500146	Escape flight, landed near Bulltofta; 27.8.45 to USSR.

Ju 52-3m remaining in Norway

Oslo-Fornebu

Ju 52-3mg4e	Works no. 2982	7U + PK T.Gr.20	Flew another 247 missions for the Norwegian Air Force.
Ju 52-3mge	Works no. 5555	OKM	Flew another 125 missions for the Norwegian Air Force.
Ju 52-3mg4e	Works no. 6048	N9 + DA	Liaison Squadron Norway, flew another 121 missions for the Norwegian Air Force.
Ju 52-3mg8e	Works no. 501196	7U + IK 2/T.Gr.20	Continued in service until 20.6.56, subsequently to Bardufoss.
Ju 52-3mg8e	Works no. 501358	7U + NL 3/T.Gr.20	Crashed on 11.8.1945 at Bardufoss.
Ju 52-3mg14e	Works no. 640066	7U + AK 2/T.Gr.20	As VM906 to Royal Air Force at Hamburg-Fuhlsbüttel.
Ju 52-3mg2e	Works no. 5489	D-AQUI DLH	Active service at Horten until 12.9.45.
Ju 52-3mg4e	Works no. 6942	8A + BK	Sea Transport Squadron 2, completely overhauled at Horten.
Ju 52-3mg8e	Works no. 501??8	8A + CK	Sea Transport Squadron 2, May 1945 to Horten for overhaul.

Gardermoen

Ju 52-3mg8e	Works no. 501219		TGr20, stayed in northern Norway during winter 1945/46.

Ju 52-3mg8e Works no. TGr20, used for spare parts.
3301
Ju 52-3mg4e Works no. RK + AV, went as VM 970 to the
5096　　　　　Royal Air Force,
　　　　　　　Hamburg-Fuhlsbüttel
Ju 52-3mg4e Works no. 7U + JK 2/T Gr.20, used for spare
6873　　　　　parts.
Drontheim
Ju 52-3mg8e Works no. 8A + AK Sea Transport Squadron 2,
3257　　　　　went to Horten in September 1945
　　　　　　　for an overhaul.
Ju 52-3mg7e Works no. Sea Transport Squadron 2,
7229　　　　　active service until June 1945, then
　　　　　　　to Horten.
JU 52-3mg8e Works no. Sea Transport Squadron 2,
130712　　　　September 1945 to Horten for an
　　　　　　　overhaul.
Ju 52-3mg8e Works no. as Works no. 130712.
130714
Hommelvik
Ju 52-3mge Works no. D-AKIQ DLH, September 1945 to
5429　　　　　Horten for an overhaul.

The Royal Air Force intended to fly a Ju 52-3mg8e of TGr 20, Works no. 5463, and a g4e of the Supreme Command of the Wehrmacht, Norway, Works no. 6171, from Gardermoen to Hamburg-Fuhlsbüttel; this was impossible because of a lack of spare parts. The machines were still at Gardermoen in May 1946.

Data Sheet for aircraft model Ju 52 1933, by the Technical Department of Reichsluftfahrtministerium

Secret!
LC　　　　　　　　　　50 copies
B.B.Nr.2763/33 0 1 g Kdos 11th copy

Preliminary data sheet for aircraft model Ju 52
1. *Application:*
Auxiliary bomber (land)

2. *Crew:*
1 Pilot
1 Commander (observer) at the same time responsible for bomb release and firing MG
1 Radio operator
1 Fuselage gunner

3. *Engines:*
Engine samples: BMW Hornet A (525 hp) and/or S 3 D1 (650 hp)

Number of engines: 3
Tank capacity:　fuel　　　2500 1)　for flight distance
　　　　　　　　lubricant　200 1)　of 1500 km

4. *Armament:*
Fuselage:
1 movable MG15, circular track 30, 13 twin magazines, 975 rounds
Pilot's cabin:
1 movable MG15, Junkers circular track, 10 twin magazines for a total of 750 rounds

5. *Bomb bay:*
Release mechanism for
a) 6 off C-250 kg bombs vertical twin suspension in the cabin,
b) 24 off C-50 kg bombs in the same devices as a), but 4 off C-50, rack plates,
c) 96 off C-10 kg bombs in the same devices and racks as b), but with 4 off C-10 suspension devices
d) 864 off 1 kg incendiary bombs and racking as b), but with 36 off E11 bomb chutes

Bomb capacity:
a) for flying distance of 1500 km: 450 kg
b) for flying distance of 1200 km: 900 kg
c) for flying distance of 1000 km: 1200 kg
d) for flying distance of 750 km: 1500 kg (maximum)
Mixed loads: as necessary, but within the limits defined by a) – d).
Aiming mechanism: Goerz F1 219b

6. *Flying weight:*
9200 kg

7. *Flying performance (only partly achieved):*
Maximum speed at low altitude:
230 km/h with Hornet A
230 km/h with Hornet S3D1
Maximum operating ceiling:　4.2 with Hornet A
　　　　　　　　　　　　　5.2 km with Hornet S3D1
Climbing time: 0 to 3 km:　20 minutes with Hornet A
　　　　　　　　　　　　　18 minutes with Hornet S3D1
Maximum range: 1500 km (at an altitude of 3-4 km, including climb and descent)
Take-off distance up to 20 m: 600 m
Landing distance from 20 m to standstill (braked): 600m
Landing speed: (at touch down) approx. 100 km/h

Bibliography

Barthélémy	Histoire du transport aérien militaire francais Edition France Empire	1981
Bekker	Angriffshöhe 4000	1964
Bongers	Es lag in der Luft	1971
Bongartz	Luftmacht Deutschland	1939
Cartier	La Seconde Guerre Mondiale	1965
Chillon, Dubois, Wegg	French postwar transport aircraft Air Britain	1980
Cuich	De l'Aéronautique Militaire 1912 à l'Armée de l'Air	1976
Chant	II. Weltkriegsflugzeuge	London 1975
Dierich	Die Verbände der Luftwaffe 1933-45	1976
Gablenz	D-ANOY bezwingt den Pamir	1937
Hahn	Deutsche Geheimwaffen 1933-45	1963
Heimann	Die Flugzeuge der Deutschen Lufthansa 1926–1980	1980
Hoyos	Pedros y Pablos	1939
Junkers	Werksprospekt Ju 52	V/61 7.31
Junkers	Werksprospekt Ju 52-3m	JFM 3926/I/39
Kössler	Transporter, wer kennt sie schon?	1976
Lange	Tante Ju	1976
Lange	Buch der deutschen Luftfahrttechnik	1972
Morzik-Hümmelchen	Die deutschen Transportflieger im II. Weltkrieg	1966
Nederlands Department van Defensie	De Luchtverdediging in de Maidagen 1940	
Nowarra	Die deutsche Luftrüstung Bd. 3	1986
Nowarra	Die verbotenen Flugzeuge 1931-35	1980
Nowarra	Luftlande-Unternehmen Norwegen April 1940	Feldgrau 1969/5
Ott	Die einmotorige Junkers Ju 52	Luftfahrt International 1980/81
Piekalkewicz	Die Ju 52 im Zweiten Weltkrieg	1976
Schramm	Kriegstagebuch des Oberkommandos der Wehrmacht 1940-45	
Supf	Buch der deutschen Fluggeschichte Bd. 2	1958
Stroud	European Transport Aircraft since 1910	1966
Thinesen	ABA und die verbesserte Ju 52-3ms	Aerokurier 6/1975
Trenkle	Die deutschen Funkstörverfahren bis 1945	1982
Völker	Die deutsche Luftwaffe 1933-39	1967
Zindel	Die Geschichte und Entwicklung des Junkers-Flugzeugbaus von 1910–1938 und bis zum endgültigen Ende 1970	DLR-Mitteilungen 79-01
Deutsche Lufthansa	Flugzeugzellen-Bestandslisten	1935-1943
Nowarra	Über Europas Fronten, Das technisch-historische Porträt der Ju 52	1978

222